CHOW HOUND

Wholesome
Home Cooking for Your
Doggie

Eve Adamson

STERLING INNOVATION
An imprint of Sterling Publishing Co., Inc.

New York / London
www.sterlingpublishing.com

STERLING, the Sterling logo, STERLING INNOVATION,
and the Sterling Innovation logo are registered trademarks of Sterling Publishing Co., Inc.

Library of Congress Cataloging-in-Publication Data Available

2 4 6 8 10 9 7 5 3 1

Published by Sterling Publishing Co., Inc.
387 Park Avenue South, New York, NY 10016
© 2009 by Sterling Publishing Co., Inc.
Distributed in Canada by Sterling Publishing
c/o Canadian Manda Group, 165 Dufferin Street
Toronto, Ontario, Canada M6K 3H6
Distributed in the United Kingdom by GMC Distribution Services
Castle Place, 166 High Street, Lewes, East Sussex, England BN7 1XU
Distributed in Australia by Capricorn Link (Australia) Pty. Ltd.
P.O. Box 704, Windsor, NSW 2756, Australia

Printed in China

Interior design by Frances Soo Ping Chow
Cover design by Melissa Gerber

Sterling ISBN 978-1-4027-5566-8

For information about custom editions, special sales, premium and
corporate purchases, please contact Sterling Special Sales
Department at 800-805-5489 or specialsales@sterlingpublishing.com.

Table of Contents

CHAPTER ONE

Why Bake for Your Dog?

~

There's something about the warmth of an oven, the smell of baking muffins or pie or cake, the process of mixing ingredients in a bowl and transforming them, like magic, into something delicious to nourish the body and soul. There's no denying it—baking has charm.

Baking is a source of comfort, and to me, baking can also promote good health. Rather than buying prepackaged treats filled with artificial ingredients and processed sweeteners, I would much rather bake something in my own kitchen.

But baking for your dog? Is that a little strange? A little obsessive? A little . . . extreme?

Absolutely not.

Dog in the Family

For many of us, our dogs become part of our families, and if you care about what your family eats, you should take a good hard look at the ingredients lists on the boxes of dog treats you've been buying. Some dog treats are well made and full of healthful ingredients, but many of them are just as junky as the processed boxes of snack cakes, cookies, and packaged muffins that you know your kids (and you!) shouldn't be eating. (You know what I'm talking about—the ones with expiration dates years down the road.)

This book is all about feeding your four-legged family members the best possible treats for their health. As an added bonus, you'll simultaneously feed your own soul by putting your love, care, and attention into the treats you bake at home. Giving your dog healthful home-baked treats is a labor of love, but the recipes in this book are so easy and fun to make that you will hardly notice the "labor" at all.

Baking for dogs is simple, because dogs don't need a lot of fancy ingredients. Dogs like basic, good, fresh food, and I created these recipes with that in mind—this book is dog-centric in its recipe formulations, and proud of it. These recipes don't call for much salt, and they leave out processed sugar altogether. And although that means you probably won't care for the taste of some of these recipes, your dog will think they taste just great. However, even if they don't all sound appetizing to you (tuna muffin, anyone?), every recipe in this book is safe for humans to eat, too. Give some of them a try—you might find a few new favorites of your own.

More Reasons to Use This Book

Because many of the recipes in this book are so simple to follow, baking these treats is a great activity to share with kids. (Just be sure you supervise any use of sharp tools or heated appliances.) These recipes can get kids interested in the joy of cooking for others and nurturing their pets in a special way. Baking for your dog just might inspire the next great chef, or even the next great veterinarian.

Baking for your dog is a fantastic way to use up leftovers, too. Many of these recipes call for precooked meat, poultry, or fish, as well as precooked grains like rice and pasta. If you have leftovers sitting around, flip through this book for ideas on how to use them. Sometimes you don't have the opportunity to use all the fresh fruits and vegetables you've purchased while they're in their prime. Rather than letting these ingredients spoil, incorporate them into baked treats for your dog. Waste not, want not!

Treats also make excellent training tools. Break the treats into smaller pieces and use them as rewards during training sessions.

Remember, however, that treats should only make up a small portion of your dog's diet. One or two treats a day is plenty for most dogs. The treats in this book are not meant to make up your dog's entire diet, and they should not exceed 10 percent of your dog's daily nutritional intake. These recipes call for fresh meats, whole grains, dairy products like plain yogurt and cottage cheese, and fruits and vegetables that are safe for dogs. However, be aware that some fruits and vegetables are toxic for dogs to eat—for a list of these and other foods you should avoid, see "Never Feed Your Dog These Foods!" on page 15.

Fresh, Delicious... and SAFE

Recently, hundreds of different brands of foods and treats for both dogs and cats were recalled because they were tainted with ingredients that made many pets very sick, sometimes fatally. Since then, there has been increased interest in making pet food and treats at home out of fear that store-bought, processed foods and treats could harm pets. But preparing your dog's entire meal can be time consuming and nutritionally tricky, and this book is not meant to guide you through that process or to provide recipes to make up your dog's complete diet.

While I'm neither a veterinarian nor a canine nutritionist, I have been writing about pet nutrition for more than a decade, and I do know this: many pet food companies make excellent food with high-quality, premium natural ingredients that provide superior nutrition for dogs. Many companies also make high-quality treats with healthful, safe ingredients.

I generally recommend that you give your dog the highest-quality pet food and treats you can afford, with the best, most natural ingredients—preferably made out of fresh meats and natural oils, with small amounts of whole grains, fruits, and vegetables. That's how dogs are meant to eat.

Make those treats at home, and *you* get to choose the ingredients. *You* control the quality, and *you* get to make them with your own hands and the love in your own heart. For special occasions, a job well done, for training, or just to show your dog how much you love him— give him a home-baked treat. Your pooch is sure to feel the love.

A Few Notes on the Recipes

Because I don't like to waste food, I've tried to help you avoid waste, too, by putting icons at the top of every recipe to show what kinds of leftovers you can use in each one. For example, every recipe that uses cooked chicken has a **chicken** icon at the top. My hope is that all of these visual cues will help make it easier for you to locate and use the recipes you want and need.

Beef   Chicken   Turkey   Pork

Fish   Veggie Dog   Grain-Free   Lamb

The icons are also helpful to owners with dogs on specialized diets. Because so many pet owners maintain grain-free diets for their dogs, this book has an entire chapter devoted to grain-free recipes—but even beyond that chapter, grain-free recipes appear throughout the book and have a **grain-free** icon. Also, there are some dogs out there who can't or don't eat meat. When a recipe doesn't contain meat, it is labeled with a **veggie dog** icon. And if your dog loves meat and digests grains just fine? No problem! I still recommend that you try some of the grain-free and meat-free recipes in this book anyway. Dogs are omni-vores (like humans) and can enjoy a whole variety of healthful foods.

When I refer to eggs in the ingredients lists, I mean large eggs, preferably organic or cage-free. Some studies show that cage-free eggs have higher levels of nutrients. Person-ally, I think they taste better. I almost always use sea salt, but occasionally kosher salt, when baking. But you can certainly use regular salt if you'd like.

Finally, whenever possible, for your dog and for yourself, I recommend you choose organic products. The fewer chemicals and pesticide residues we put into ourselves and our dogs, the better, I say—even if science has yet to definitively prove it. The choice is yours, of course.

TO WHEAT OR
NOT TO WHEAT?

Although vets say food allergies are much less common in dogs than some people think, many dogs are either allergic or sensitive to wheat and corn. Dogs aren't really designed to eat a lot of grain—your dog chases squirrels and rabbits, but have you ever seen her hunting a corn stalk? Of course not.

Some dogs do just fine with whole grains as part of their diets (though no dog should be eating white flour or sugar), but others tend to have skin reactions if they eat too much wheat and corn. If wheat and/or corn don't agree with your dog, take a cue from the gluten-free human community and use brown rice flour, amaranth flour, millet flour, and other alternative grains when cooking for your dog. Alternative flours cost more than wheat flour, but for many people who already eat gluten-free, they are the only way to bake. More and more grocery stores carry them, too.

Because most alternative flours lack gluten—the sticky stuff in wheat that helps baked goods hold their shape—you may need to use an extra egg or xanthan gum (a powder that stands in for gluten in baking) in your recipes if you don't want them to fall apart. Then again, remember your audience—your dog probably won't care if her favorite fish muffins get a little bit crumbly.

If you don't know whether your dog is sensitive to wheat and/or corn, just remember that no dog should eat a lot of grains. Limit grain-based treats to less than 10 percent of your dog's daily food intake, and chances are that she'll be fine. If your dog experiences itching, rashes, or other skin discomforts, talk to your veterinarian about the possibility of a food sensitivity and try focusing your cooking efforts on the grain-free treats in Chapter Ten to see if that makes a difference.

CHAPTER TWO

The Basics: Equipment, Supplies, and Pantry Staples

~

You don't need a whole lot of stuff to start cooking for your pooch, but before you tie on your apron and dip your hands into the flour bin, let's go over the basic tools and ingredients you'll need to get started on the recipes in this book. Even if you maintain a well-stocked pantry, always check the recipe before you start, to confirm you have all the supplies and ingredients you need.

Equipment and Supplies

Most of the recipes in this book require an oven, and some of them require a stovetop or a microwave. I'm going to assume that you have these things. Unless you are strong and like to beat stuff by hand, you also need an electric mixer. A food processor and a blender aren't absolutely necessary, but they can make some of these recipes easier to prepare.

You will also need the following baking supplies:

- **Muffin tin** (standard-sized and/or mini). If you have a large dog (more than 40 pounds), standard muffins are about right. For a dog less than 40 pounds, however, mini muffin tins are perfect. Just because your dog *will* eat a big muffin treat doesn't mean he *should*.

- **Loaf pan** (standard-sized and/or mini). Since you will cut loaves into pieces, it doesn't matter what size you use, but if you know you won't go through treats very quickly, use the mini pans. You can always freeze extra loaves for future use.
- **9-inch pie plate**
- **8-inch round cake pan**
- **13 x 9–inch cake pan**
- **Baking sheets** (also known as cookie sheets)
- **Nonstick baking mat** (such as Silpat) or parchment paper
- **Ceramic ramekins** or **ovenproof custard cups** (standard-sized and/or mini). Again, use the standard sizes for dogs more than 40 pounds, the mini sizes for dogs less than 40 pounds.
- **Wire cooling rack**
- **Various standard kitchen utensils:** Wooden or plastic spoons, whisk, spatula, toothpicks for testing doneness
- **Biscuit cutters** (standard-sized and/or mini, depending on your dog's size), or use a wine glass for standard-sized biscuits and a shot glass for mini biscuits
- **Bone-shaped cookie cutter**, or cut by freehand

Pantry Staples

This list includes the essential ingredients you will need for making the recipes in this book. Keep your pantry well stocked so you can start baking whenever the mood strikes. I recommend choosing organic ingredients, whenever possible.

Dry Goods
Baking powder
Baking soda
Barley
Barley flour
Brown rice
Brown rice flour
Carob chips
Carob powder
Coconut, flaked or shredded (unsweetened)

Cornmeal (yellow or white)

Gluten-free baking mix

Millet flour

Oats, rolled (*old-fashioned oats* or *quick-cooking oats*)

Pasta, whole grain (such as whole wheat, brown rice, or quinoa)

Quinoa (a delicious, high-protein grain available in health food stores and, increasingly, in regular supermarkets)

Sea salt and/or kosher salt

Soy flour

Tapioca starch

Whole-wheat pastry flour (or read labels to find a whole-wheat flour that will work for baking)

Xanthan gum (optional, but using will produce better results when baking with gluten-free flours)

Yeast, brewer's or nutritional (not baking or bread yeast)

Nuts, Seeds, and Oils

Almond meal (or almonds you can grind yourself)

Canola oil

Flaxseed oil or hemp oil

Flaxseeds, ground (or whole flaxseeds you can grind yourself)

Olive oil (extra-virgin)

Peanut butter, natural (creamy)

Peanut oil

Sesame butter (also called *tahini)*

Meat, Poultry, Fish, Eggs, and Dairy

Fresh or frozen meat of all kinds, whole, deboned, and ground. (Stock up when meat goes on sale. Whenever you cook a whole chicken, turkey, or duck, save the liver and other organs and freeze them for later use—they'll make great additions to your dog's baked treats.)

Baby food (strained beef, chicken, and turkey)

Beef

Butter

Cheddar cheese

Chicken (including organs)

Chicken, canned

Cottage cheese (preferably low-sodium, part-skim)

Duck (including organs)

Eggs (large)

Fish (such as salmon, cod, and halibut)

Ham (low-sodium)

Lamb

Parmesan cheese

Pork

Rabbit

Ricotta cheese (part skim)
Tuna, canned (water packed)
Turkey (including organs)
Wild game meats (such as venison, elk,
and pheasant)
Yogurt, nonfat plain

Fresh Produce
Apples
Bananas
Blueberries
Broccoli
Carrots
Green beans
Greens (such as collard greens, mustard
greens, and kale)
Kelp, dried
Peas
Potatoes
Seaweed, dried (also called *nori*)
Strawberries
Sweet potatoes

Herbs and Spices (Dried and Fresh)
Basil
Cumin
Ginger, ground
Ginger root
Oregano
Paprika
Thyme

Miscellaneous Ingredients
Applesauce, unsweetened (natural)
Broth, beef (low-sodium, in a can or box)
Broth, chicken (low-sodium, in a can or box)
Broth, turkey (low-sodium, in a can or box)
Pumpkin puree, canned (plain, *not* pumpkin
pie mix)
Honey
Molasses
Soy sauce (low-sodium, also called *tamari*)

NEVER FEED YOUR DOG THESE FOODS!

A few foods that humans tolerate just fine are toxic to dogs, causing symptoms ranging from mild stomach discomfort to organ failure and even death. While some dogs might be able to handle some of these ingredients in small amounts, there is no good reason to take the risk. To protect your dog, never include any of the following ingredients in anything you plan to feed him:

Alcoholic beverages of any kind

Avocado

Chocolate (especially baking chocolate)

Coffee (the caffeine can be deadly)

Fruit seeds and pits (especially from apples, cherries, peaches, pears, plums, or apricots)

Garlic (fresh)

Grapes and raisins

Mushrooms

Nutmeg (don't be tempted to add it to your baked goods!)

Nuts (especially walnuts and macadamias)

Onions

Sugarless gum or candy (the artificial sweetener xylitol is the culprit)

Tea

Tomatoes

Uncooked dough

CHAPTER THREE

Amazing Muffins

~

Fun to bake, warm, and homey, muffins practically ooze comfort, and now your dog can enjoy them, too. Muffins are perfect dog treats because they're already portioned into bite-sized morsels. But these muffins aren't like the chocolate chip or apple cinnamon or banana nut muffin you might eat for breakfast. Your dog needs a slightly different set of ingredients. Because a large amount of grain isn't a good nutritional choice for dogs, these muffins tend to be dense and meaty or eggy, rather than fluffy and full of flour. Trust me, your dog will like them better this way.

In fact, I'm guessing the protein-rich, full-fiber muffins in this chapter will make your dog very happy. For dogs who weigh less than 40 pounds, use mini muffin tins or cut muffins into quarters or halves. And remember: no more than one per day. (OK, two max!)

Muffins freeze well, so if a whole batch won't be eaten within four or five days, pop the remaining muffins into a freezer bag and store them in the freezer. You can defrost one in the microwave whenever your dog deserves a special treat.

Chicken Little Muffins

Makes 6 regular or 12 mini muffins

Is your dog barking like the sky is falling? Calm her down with one of these delectable muffins. She'll soon be deliciously distracted.

1 cup shredded cooked chicken
1 cup nonfat plain yogurt
1 tablespoon ground flaxseeds
1 cup whole-wheat pastry flour
½ teaspoon baking soda
½ teaspoon cumin
1 teaspoon dried oregano
1 teaspoon dried basil

1. Preheat the oven to 350 degrees. Coat a regular or mini muffin tin with cooking spray, or line with paper liners.

2. Combine the chicken, yogurt, and flaxseeds in a large bowl.

3. In a separate bowl, combine the flour, baking soda, cumin, oregano, and basil. Add the dry ingredients to the chicken mixture and stir just until combined.

4. Spoon the mixture into the prepared muffin tin. Bake for 20 minutes for regular muffins, about 12 minutes for mini muffins, or until the muffins feel firm to the touch. Let cool for 15 minutes, then remove the muffins from the tin and serve. Refrigerate leftovers in an airtight container for up to 2 days, or freeze for up to 2 months.

Cheeseburger Muffins

Makes 6 regular or 12 mini muffins

These muffins are like mini cheeseburgers without the bun. *You* might even like them!

1 cup cooked ground beef
½ cup rolled oats
½ cup whole-wheat pastry flour
½ teaspoon baking soda
1 egg
½ cup shredded Cheddar cheese

1. Preheat the oven to 350 degrees. Spray a regular or mini muffin tin with cooking spray, or line with paper liners.

2. In a large bowl, combine the ground beef, rolled oats, flour, baking soda, and egg until all the ingredients are well incorporated.

3. Spoon the beef mixture into the prepared muffin tin and sprinkle the cheese evenly over each cup. Bake for 20 minutes for regular muffins, about 12 minutes for mini muffins, or until lightly browned. Let cool for 15 minutes, then remove the muffins from the tin and serve. Refrigerate leftovers in an airtight container for up to 2 days, or freeze for up to 2 months.

Egg-Zactly Muffins

Makes 6 regular or 12 mini muffins

These eggy muffins are almost like mini quiches and make a delicious breakfast for dogs or people.

1 cup cooked rice (brown or white)

1 teaspoon olive oil

2 eggs

½ cup milk

½ cup chopped low-sodium ham

1. Preheat the oven to 400 degrees. Spray a regular or mini muffin tin with cooking spray, or line with paper liners.

2. Scoop an equal portion of rice into each muffin cup. Rub the olive oil on your fingers, then press the rice into the bottom and just slightly up the sides of each cup.

3. In a small bowl, beat the eggs, milk, and ham together.

4. Pour the mixture evenly into the prepared muffin tin. Bake for 20 minutes for regular muffins, about 12 minutes for mini muffins—or until the egg is cooked through. Let cool for 15 minutes, then remove the muffins from the tin with a fork or a small spatula. Serve immediately. Refrigerate leftovers in an airtight container for up to 2 days, or freeze for up to 2 months.

Hush Puppy Fish Muffins

Makes 6 regular or 12 mini muffins

These fish-filled muffins are reminiscent of fish cakes.

½ cup fresh or low-sodium canned, drained flaked fish (like tuna)

½ cup cornmeal

½ cup whole-wheat pastry flour

1 egg
2 tablespoons canola oil
½ cup low-sodium meat, fish, or vegetable broth, or water
¼ teaspoon paprika

1. Preheat the oven to 400 degrees. Spray a regular or mini muffin tin with cooking spray, or line with paper liners.

2. In a large bowl, mix together the fish, cornmeal, and flour.

3. In a separate bowl, mix together the egg, canola oil, broth or water, and paprika. Add the wet ingredients to the dry and toss gently with a fork until just combined.

4. Spoon the batter into the prepared muffin tin. Bake for 20 minutes for regular muffins, about 12 minutes for mini muffins—or until the tops start to turn golden brown. Let cool for 15 minutes, then remove the muffins from the tin and serve. Refrigerate leftovers in an airtight container for up to 2 days, or freeze for up to 2 months.

Carrot Applesauce Muffins

Makes 6 regular or 12 mini muffins

These fruity and fiber-rich muffins aren't full of sugar, so people might not care for them. Dogs, on the other hand, are likely to find them delicious.

½ cup unsweetened applesauce

3 tablespoons canola oil

2 eggs, beaten

1 cup brown rice flour

¼ cup ground flaxseeds

½ teaspoon baking soda

½ teaspoon baking powder

1 cup shredded carrots

¼ teaspoon cinnamon

1. Preheat the oven to 350 degrees. Spray a regular or mini muffin tin with cooking spray, or line with paper liners.

2. In a large bowl, stir together the applesauce, canola oil, eggs, flour, flaxseeds, baking soda, baking powder, carrots, and cinnamon. Mix with a fork until well combined.

3. Spoon the batter into the prepared muffin tins. Bake for 20 minutes for regular muffins, about 12 minutes for mini muffins—or until the tops start to turn golden brown. Let cool for 15 minutes, then remove the muffins from the tin and serve. Refrigerate leftovers in an airtight container for up to 4 days, or freeze for up to 4 months.

Turkey Quinoa Muffins

Makes 6 regular or 12 mini muffins

Quinoa looks like a grain, but it is actually a nutritionally dense, high-protein, low-carbohydrate grass seed. It's super healthful for pets and people.

1 cup quinoa
½ cup chopped or shredded cooked turkey
½ cup nonfat plain yogurt
1 egg
2 tablespoons whole-wheat pastry flour
½ teaspoon baking powder
1 tablespoon melted butter
1 tablespoon grated Parmesan cheese

1. Preheat the oven to 350 degrees. Spray a regular or mini muffin tin with cooking spray, or line with paper liners.

2. In a large bowl, mix together the quinoa, turkey, yogurt, egg, flour, baking powder, butter, and Parmesan cheese until well combined.

3. Spoon the batter into the prepared muffin tin. Bake for 20 minutes for regular muffins, about 12 minutes for mini muffins—or until the tops start to turn golden brown. Let cool for 15 minutes, then remove the muffins from the tin and serve. Refrigerate leftovers in an airtight container for up to 2 days, or freeze for up to 2 months.

Triple B Muffins

Makes 6 regular or 12 mini muffins

These muffins contain three highly nutritious foods with names that begin with the letter B: *beef*, *broccoli*, and *barley*. The barley can be instant, cooked according to the package directions.

1½ cups cooked barley
½ cup chopped or shredded cooked beef
¼ cup pureed cooked broccoli
1 tablespoon sesame seeds

2 eggs

½ teaspoon ground ginger,
or 1 teaspoon finely grated fresh ginger root

¼ teaspoon low-sodium soy sauce (optional)

1. Preheat the oven to 400 degrees. Spray a regular or mini muffin tin with cooking spray, or line with paper liners.

2. In a large bowl, mix together the barley, beef, broccoli, sesame seeds, eggs, ginger, and soy sauce (if using). Stir until well combined.

3. Spoon the batter into the prepared muffin tins. Bake for 20 minutes for regular muffins, about 12 minutes for mini muffins—or until the tops start to turn golden brown. Let cool for 15 minutes, then remove the muffins from the tin and serve. Refrigerate leftovers in an airtight container for up to 2 days, or freeze for up to 2 months.

Cottage Cheese Surprise Muffins

Makes 6 regular or 12 mini muffins

These fiber-rich bran muffins have a creamy cottage cheese center—a nice surprise for your dog to bite into. You may substitute ½ cup low-sodium chicken broth for the water called for in this recipe if your dog's diet includes meat.

½ cup oat bran
¼ cup ground flaxseeds
2 tablespoons canola oil
1 egg
½ cup water
½ cup whole-wheat pastry flour
½ teaspoon baking soda
6 tablespoons low-fat cottage cheese

1. Preheat the oven to 375 degrees. Spray a regular or mini muffin tin with cooking spray, or line with paper liners.

2. In a large bowl, mix together the oat bran, flaxseeds, canola oil, egg, and ½ cup water until well combined.

3. In a smaller bowl, combine the flour and baking soda. Add the dry ingredients to the wet ingredients and mix just until combined.

4. Spoon half the batter into the muffin tins, filling each cup about ⅓ of the way full. Drop 1 tablespoon cottage cheese (for regular muffins) or ½ tablespoon cottage cheese (for mini muffins) in the middle of each muffin, then cover with the remaining batter. Bake for 20 minutes for regular muffins, about 12 minutes for mini muffins—or until the tops start to turn golden brown. Let cool for 15 minutes, then carefully remove the muffins from the tin and serve. Refrigerate leftovers in an airtight container for up to 2 days, or freeze for up to 2 months.

Blueberry Sweet Potato Muffins

Makes 6 regular or 12 mini muffins

Blueberries and sweet potatoes might sound like a strange taste combination to you, but these two ingredients are among the most potent nutritional powerhouses in the plant kingdom. You might even want to try the combination yourself.

1 egg
¼ cup canola oil
1 tablespoon flaxseed or hemp oil (optional)

½ cup whole-wheat pastry flour

½ cup cornmeal

1 teaspoon baking powder

½ teaspoon cinnamon

½ cup nonfat plain yogurt

¾ cup peeled, grated sweet potato

¼ cup ground almonds

½ cup mashed fresh or frozen (defrosted) blueberries

1. Preheat the oven to 375 degrees. Spray a regular or mini muffin tin with cooking spray, or line with paper liners.

2. In a large bowl, mix together the egg, canola oil, and flaxseed or hemp oil (if using).

3. In a separate bowl, combine the flour, cornmeal, baking powder, and cinnamon. Mix until well combined. Add the dry ingredients to the oil mixture along with the yogurt, sweet potato, almonds, and blueberries. Mix lightly until all ingredients are just combined.

4. Spoon the batter into the prepared muffin tin. Bake for 20 minutes for regular muffins, about 12 minutes for mini muffins—or until the tops start to turn golden brown. Let cool for 15 minutes, then remove the muffins from the tin and serve. Refrigerate leftovers in an airtight container for up to 2 days, or freeze for up to 2 months.

CHAPTER FOUR

Pies for Pooches

~

You know what they say: Everybody loves pie. That goes for dogs, too, as long as the pie is full of delicious, healthful, dog-friendly ingredients. But because dogs don't need very much pie for a treat—a thin slice or scoop will be plenty—these recipes work best for households with lots of dogs (or with people who will eat them, too), or for special dog events like doggy playdates and parties.

Take a pooch pie to your local animal shelter or the grand opening of a boutique pet store that lets dogs visit. Give pies as gifts to dog-owning friends. You'll have plenty to save or share, because one pie serves about 12 large dogs or 24 small ones.

These recipes are designed for 9-inch pie plates. Store-bought crusts are guaranteed not to give you any trouble, but if you are a piecrust whiz, feel free to substitute your favorite piecrust recipe for any of the yummies in this chapter. One warning, however: whole-grain crusts are better for dogs' health. Avoid feeding them too many (if any) foods containing white flour.

Turkey Pot Pie

Makes 12 regular or 24 small treats

This classic comfort food tastes even better when it's homemade. You might think it needs more salt, but your dog should enjoy this mild-tasting version. Kids might like it, too—the vegetables are mashed up, so even picky eaters will hardly notice them.

1 (9-inch) frozen or refrigerated whole-wheat deep-dish pie shell for 2-crust pie
2 cups cubed or shredded cooked turkey
1 cup cooked mixed vegetables, or canned mixed vegetables, drained
1 cup shredded, sliced, or diced cooked potatoes
2 cups low-sodium chicken or turkey broth
½ teaspoon dried or 1 teaspoon chopped fresh sage
½ teaspoon cumin
1 tablespoon cornstarch

1. Thaw the pie shell (if frozen) according to package instructions.

2. Preheat the oven to 400 degrees.

3. In a large skillet over medium-high heat, combine the turkey, vegetables, potatoes, broth, sage, and cumin. Cook, stirring occasionally, until the mixture simmers and the vegetables get soft, about 15 minutes. As the mixture cooks, mash up the vegetables and potatoes with a fork so

you don't have any large vegetable pieces. Continue to simmer until the liquid has reduced by about half.

4. Combine the cornstarch with 2 tablespoons water to form a paste. Add the cornstarch paste to the skillet and stir constantly until the mixture thickens to the consistency of gravy.

5. Pour the turkey mixture into the pie shell and assemble the top crust according to the package directions. Bake for 10 minutes, then remove the pie from the oven and cover the edges with foil to prevent over-browning. Return the pie to the oven and bake for an additional 40 minutes, or until the pie filling is hot and bubbling.

6. Remove from the oven and allow the pie to cool on a rack for 30 minutes to an hour before serving. Serve warm or at room temperature. Store leftovers covered in the refrigerator for up to 2 days, or sealed in an airtight container for up to 1 month in the freezer.

Baked Taco Pie

Makes enough for 12 regular or 24 small treats

You don't need to have a Chihuahua to make this yummy Mexican-inspired pie, filled with dog-friendly ingredients.

8 (6-inch) corn tortillas
1 cup nonfat plain yogurt
1 pound lean ground beef, cooked and drained
4 eggs
¼ cup low-sodium chicken broth or water
½ cup finely shredded Cheddar cheese

1. Preheat the oven to 400 degrees.

2. Wrap the tortillas in a damp paper towel and heat them in the microwave on high for 1 minute to soften. While they are still warm, arrange them over the bottom and sides of a 9-inch pie plate to form a crust.

3. Spread the yogurt on the bottom of the tortilla crust, then evenly distribute the ground beef on top of the yogurt.

4. In a small bowl, combine the eggs and the chicken broth or water. Mix well.

5. Pour the egg mixture over the ground beef in the pie plate. Bake the pie for 45 minutes, then remove it from the oven and sprinkle the cheese

evenly on the top. Return the pie to the oven and bake for an additional 10 minutes, or until the cheese melts.

6. Remove the pie from the oven and allow it to cool on a rack for 30 minutes to an hour before serving. Serve warm or at room temperature. Store leftovers covered in the refrigerator for up to 2 days, or sealed in an airtight container for up to 1 month in the freezer.

Savory Chicken Apple Pie

Makes enough for 12 regular or 24 small treats

What does your dog think is missing in that good old-fashioned apple pie? Why, a little chicken, of course! You may think this pie sounds strange, but try it. You might even like it.

1 (9-inch) frozen or refrigerated whole-wheat deep-dish pie shell for 2-crust pie

2 Granny Smith apples

1 tablespoon freshly squeezed lemon juice

2 tablespoons cornstarch or tapioca starch

2 cups diced or shredded cooked chicken

¼ cup molasses

½ cup unsweetened apple juice or cider

½ teaspoon cinnamon

1. Thaw the pie shell (if frozen) according to package instructions.

2. Preheat the oven to 400 degrees.

3. Peel, core, and thinly slice the apples. Toss the slices with the lemon juice, then sprinkle 1 tablespoon of the cornstarch (or tapioca starch) on the slices and toss to coat. Arrange half of the apple slices in the pie shell. Set the remaining half aside.

4. In a large bowl, combine the chicken, molasses, apple juice or cider, cinnamon, and the remaining tablespoon of cornstarch (or tapioca starch). Stir until mixed.

5. Pour the chicken mixture over the apples in the pie shell. Top with the remaining apple slices, and assemble the top crust according to the package directions. Bake for 15 minutes, then remove the pie from the oven and cover the edges with foil to prevent over-browning. Return the pie to the oven and bake an additional 45 minutes, or until the crust is a deep golden brown.

6. Remove the pie from the oven and allow it to cool on a rack for 30 minutes to an hour before serving. Serve warm or at room temperature. Store leftovers covered in the refrigerator for up to 2 days, or sealed in an airtight container for up to 1 month in the freezer.

Sheepdog Pie

Makes enough for 12 regular or 24 small treats

This is my version of a classic shepherd's pie, but of course, this one is for the sheepdog. This recipe contains lamb, for although sheepdogs tradition-ally guarded the sheep, those same sheep and lambs were an important source of food, too. If you prefer, substitute beef for the lamb.

1 tablespoon olive oil
1 pound ground or diced lamb, cooked
2 carrots, grated
1 celery stalk, finely minced
1 teaspoon dried or 1 tablespoon fresh chopped oregano
½ teaspoon garlic powder
2 cups mashed potatoes, or 2 cooked potatoes, thinly sliced
½ teaspoon paprika

1. Preheat the oven to 375 degrees. Rub the olive oil all over the inside surface of a 9-inch pie plate.

2. In a large bowl, combine the lamb, carrots, celery, oregano, and garlic powder.

3. Transfer the mixture directly into the pie plate, pressing it down slightly to mold it into shape. Spread the mashed potatoes on top, or if using sliced potatoes, arrange the slices to cover. Sprinkle the potatoes with

paprika. Bake for 1 hour, or until you can hear the meat sizzling and the potatoes have turned golden brown.

4. Remove the pie from the oven and cool on a rack for 30 minutes to an hour before serving. Serve warm or at room temperature. Store leftovers covered in the refrigerator for up to 2 days, or sealed in an airtight container for up to 1 month in the freezer.

Very Veggie Pie

Makes enough for 12 regular or 24 small treats

For this pie, just press cooked rice into a greased pie plate for a yummy crust that's easy as, well, *pie*. You can use any veggie stew in this recipe, as long as it doesn't contain onions, which can cause a toxic reaction in some dogs. Just be sure all the veggies are cut or grated into very small pieces to assure easy digestion. You can also whiz them all in a food processor or blender.

2 tablespoons olive oil
3 cups cooked rice (the stickier, the better)
Canola oil, for greasing fingers (optional)
1 medium zucchini, grated

1 medium sweet potato, peeled and grated
½ cup finely chopped broccoli and/or cauliflower florets
2 carrots, grated
1 celery stalk, finely minced
1 teaspoon dried or 1 tablespoon chopped fresh basil
½ teaspoon sea salt

1. Preheat the oven to 375 degrees. Coat a 9-inch pie plate with 1 tablespoon of the olive oil.

2. Press the rice into the bottom and up the sides of the pie plate to form a crust. If the rice sticks to your fingers, coat them with canola oil.

3. In a large bowl, combine the zucchini, sweet potato, broccoli and/or cauliflower, carrots, celery, basil, and salt. Pour the mixture into the rice crust. Drizzle the pie with the remaining tablespoon of olive oil. Bake for 1 hour, or until the vegetables are lightly browned.

4. Remove the pie from the oven and allow it to cool on a rack for 30 minutes to an hour before serving. Serve warm or at room temperature. Store leftovers covered in the refrigerator for up to 2 days, or sealed in an airtight container for up to 1 month in the freezer.

Breakfast Buffet Pie

Makes enough for 12 regular or 24 small treats

Normally, I don't recommend giving dogs bacon and sausage, but a little low-sodium bacon or turkey bacon makes this pie (it's really more of a *strata*) a special once-in-awhile treat. You can mix up this pie the night before and keep it in the refrigerator, covered, until morning. Just pop it in the oven, bake it until it's golden brown, and breakfast is served.

1 teaspoon canola oil

2 slices whole-wheat or sprouted grain bread

½ cup low-fat cottage cheese or part-skim ricotta cheese

4 eggs

½ cup nonfat milk

2 slices cooked low-sodium bacon or turkey bacon,
crumbled or chopped into small pieces

1. Coat a 9-inch pie plate with the canola oil.

2. Break the bread into small (less than 1-inch) pieces and put the pieces into the pie plate. Drop small globs of cottage or ricotta cheese evenly onto the bread.

3. In a medium-sized bowl, beat together the eggs and milk. Stir in the bacon pieces. Carefully pour the egg mixture into the pie plate over

the bread and cheese. Cover with plastic wrap and refrigerate for at least 2 hours, or overnight.

4. Preheat the oven to 350 degrees. Remove the plastic wrap and bake the pie for 40 minutes, or until golden brown and the eggs are set.

5. Remove the pie from the oven and allow it to cool on a rack for 30 minutes to an hour before serving. Serve warm or at room temperature. Store leftovers covered in the refrigerator for up to 2 days, or sealed in an airtight container for up to 1 month in the freezer.

———————

Potato Cheese Pie

Makes enough for 12 regular or 24 small treats

Love potatoes? You might have to argue with your dog over who gets to eat the leftovers. If your pooch isn't a vegetarian, you can add a layer of chopped low-sodium ham, shredded chicken, or cooked ground beef to the middle of this pie.

1 tablespoon canola oil
1 cup low-fat cottage cheese
1 cup mashed silken tofu
3 cups cooked (or defrosted) hash brown potatoes

½ cup finely grated Cheddar cheese

¼ cup finely grated Parmesan cheese

1 teaspoon paprika

1. Preheat the oven to 400 degrees. Coat a 9-inch pie plate with canola oil.

2. In a medium-sized bowl, mash the cottage cheese and tofu together with a fork until well combined.

3. Put 1 cup of the hash browns into the bottom of the pie plate. Top with 1 cup of the cottage cheese/tofu mixture and ¼ cup of the Cheddar cheese. Layer with another cup of hash browns, the remaining cottage cheese/tofu mixture, and the remaining ¼ cup Cheddar cheese. Top with the remaining cup of hash browns and press down with your hands to solidify. Sprinkle the top with the Parmesan cheese and paprika. Bake the pie for 40 minutes, or until the pie turns golden brown and is heated through.

4. Remove the pie from the oven and allow it to cool on a rack for 20 minutes to an hour before serving. Serve warm or at room temperature. Store leftovers covered in the refrigerator for up to 2 days, or in a sealed airtight container in the freezer for up to 1 month.

Here Kitty, Kitty Tuna Pie

Makes enough for 12 regular or 24 small treats

Cats might come running when they smell this fishy pie. Feel free to give your cat a tiny slice, too. But remember, this is just a treat, not a whole meal! Note: If you want to make this pie grain-free, just leave off the bread crumbs.

1 tablespoon olive oil

2 eggs

½ cup low-sodium chicken broth

1 ½ pounds cooked tuna, or 2 (6-ounce) cans low-sodium tuna, drained

2 tablespoons dried or ¼ cup chopped fresh parsley

½ cup whole-grain bread crumbs

1. Preheat the oven to 400 degrees. Coat a 9-inch pie plate with olive oil.

2. In a medium-sized bowl, beat together the eggs and chicken broth. Stir in the tuna and parsley.

3. Pour the mixture into the pie plate, and sprinkle the bread crumbs evenly over the top. Bake the pie for 45 minutes, or until the eggs are set and the bread crumbs turn golden brown.

4. Remove the pie from the oven and allow it to cool on a rack for 30 minutes to an hour before serving. Serve warm or at room temperature. Store leftovers covered in the refrigerator for up to 2 days, or sealed in an airtight container for up to 1 month in the freezer.

CHAPTER FIVE

Canine Quick Breads

~

Quick breads are fun to make because they give you such a delicious reward for so little effort. If you've made quick breads in the past, they were probably sweet, but most of the breads in this chapter are savory. Who says you can't put meat in a quick bread? The recipes in this chapter prove that you most certainly can—and your dog will be glad you did.

For smaller dogs, cut the loaf into slices, then cut the slices into strips or cubes. Or cut the whole loaf into cubes and freeze them, thawing just as much as you need each time. These quick breads also make great gifts for your dog-loving friends. Wrap them in tinted cellophane and tie them with a ribbon.

You can make these recipes in a standard 9 x 5–inch loaf pan or in two mini loaf pans. The minis are nice because you can keep one and give one to a friend. Or, if you only have one or two small dogs, halve any of these recipes to make one mini loaf.

Meatloaf "Bread"

Makes I regular loaf or 2 mini loaves (enough for about 12 regular or 24 small treats)

This isn't exactly *bread*, but you do bake it in a bread pan—so I say, close enough! Besides, what dog can resist a slice of meatloaf? This version makes a delicious and healthy treat for your dog, and unlike most meatloaf, it's onion-free, making it dog friendly.

2 pounds lean ground beef

I cup rolled oats

½ cup Parmesan cheese

I carrot, grated

¼ cup low-sodium beef or chicken broth

½ teaspoon garlic powder

1. Preheat the oven to 350 degrees. Coat a loaf pan with cooking spray.

2. In a large bowl, combine the ground beef, rolled oats, Parmesan cheese, carrot, broth, and garlic powder. Mix with your hands until well combined.

3. Press the mixture into the prepared loaf pan. Bake for 1 hour, or about 30 minutes for mini loaves—or until the internal temperature of the meatloaf reaches 160 degrees on a meat thermometer.

4. Remove the loaf from the oven and cool on a rack for at least 15 minutes before serving. Serve warm or at room temperature. Store leftovers in the refrigerator for up to 2 days, or freeze for up to 1 month.

Peanut Butter Pooch Bread

Makes 1 regular loaf or 2 mini loaves (enough for about 12 regular or 24 small treats)

Your kids might like this bread as much as your dogs like it. Pass the plate around; it's healthy for everyone. Be sure to use natural (unsweetened) peanut butter.

2 cups whole-wheat pastry flour

1 teaspoon baking soda

½ teaspoon sea salt

1 cup creamy natural peanut butter

½ cup canola oil

½ cup honey

2 eggs

2 large ripe bananas, mashed

2 teaspoons cider or white vinegar

1. Preheat the oven to 350 degrees. Coat a loaf pan with cooking spray.

2. In a large bowl, combine the flour, baking soda, and salt. Stir in the peanut butter, canola oil, honey, and eggs and beat with an electric mixer on medium speed until well combined, about 3 minutes. Stir in the bananas and vinegar.

3. Pour the batter into the prepared loaf pan and bake for 1 hour, or about 30 minutes for mini loaves—or until a toothpick inserted into the center comes out clean. Cool on a rack for 15 minutes, then remove from the pan. Slice and serve warm or at room temperature. Store leftovers in the refrigerator for up to 4 days, or freeze for up to 3 months.

Thyme-ly Terrier Tea Bread

Makes 1 regular loaf or 2 mini loaves
(enough for about 12 regular or 24 small treats)

This thyme-scented, breath-freshening herb bread
also contains anise, a flavor dogs absolutely love.

2 cups whole-wheat pastry flour

1 cup brown rice flour

1 tablespoon baking powder

½ teaspoon sea salt

2 eggs

1 cup nonfat plain yogurt

½ cup olive oil

¼ cup finely chopped fresh thyme, or 2 tablespoons dried

¼ cup finely chopped fresh parsley

2 tablespoons anise seeds

1. Preheat the oven to 350 degrees. Spray a loaf pan with cooking spray.

2. In a large bowl, combine the whole-wheat flour, brown rice flour, baking powder, and salt.

3. In a separate bowl, combine the eggs, yogurt, and olive oil, mixing well. Add the egg mixture to the dry ingredients and stir until just combined. Stir in the thyme, parsley and anise.

4. Pour the batter into the prepared loaf pan. Bake for 45 minutes, or about 25 minutes for mini loaves—or until a toothpick inserted into the center comes out clean. Cool on a rack for 15 minutes, then remove from the pan. Slice and serve warm or at room temperature. Store leftovers in the refrigerator for up to 4 days, or freeze for up to 3 months.

Paw-Print Potato Bread

Makes 1 regular loaf or 2 mini loaves
(enough for about 12 regular or 24 small treats)

This yummy bread is similar to Irish potato bread, though it is baked rather than fried on a griddle. You can bake it in a loaf pan as directed below, or on a baking sheet, shaped into the traditional round loaves that can be cut into strips or wedges after baking. (Bake round loaves for about ¾ of the recommended time.) The tofu adds protein to this carbohydrate-rich treat—although tofu is certainly not a traditional ingredient in Irish potato bread!

2 cups mashed potatoes
2 cups rolled oats, pulverized in the blender into oat flour
½ teaspoon sea salt
1 egg
1 cup mashed silken tofu
½ cup canola oil

1. Preheat the oven to 350 degrees. Spray a loaf pan with cooking spray.

2. Combine the mashed potatoes, pulverized oats, and salt until the oats are thoroughly incorporated into the potatoes.

3. In a medium-sized bowl, beat the egg, then add the tofu and canola oil. Pour the tofu mixture into the potato mixture and stir until fully combined.

4. Press the batter into a loaf pan and smooth the top. Bake for 45 minutes, about 25 minutes for mini loaves—or until the top turns golden brown. Cool on a rack for 15 minutes, then remove from the pan. Slice and serve warm or at room temperature. Store leftovers in the refrigerator for up to 4 days, or freeze for up to 3 months.

Berries-and-Cream Bread

Makes 1 regular loaf or 2 mini loaves (enough for about 12 regular or 24 small treats)

This berry bread is rich in cancer-fighting antioxidants. It probably won't charm dogs who only like meaty dishes, but many dogs will think it's just delicious. Try it out—even if your dog doesn't like it, you probably will.

1 cup whole-wheat pastry flour
½ cup brown rice flour
½ cup cornmeal
1 tablespoon baking powder

1 teaspoon baking soda
½ teaspoon sea salt
3 eggs
½ cup unsweetened applesauce
½ cup canola oil
⅔ cup honey
2 tablespoons molasses
2 cups mixed berries (defrosted, if frozen)

1. Preheat the oven to 350 degrees. Spray a loaf pan with cooking spray.

2. In a large bowl, combine the whole-wheat flour, brown rice flour, cornmeal, baking powder, baking soda, and sea salt.

3. In a separate bowl, beat the eggs lightly, then add the applesauce, canola oil, honey, and molasses. Add the egg mixture to the flour mixture and stir just until combined (it will be lumpy). Gently stir in the berries.

4. Pour the batter into the loaf pan. Bake for 1 hour, or about 30 minutes for mini loaves—or until a toothpick inserted into the center comes out clean. Cool on a rack for 15 minutes, then remove from the pan. Slice and serve warm or at room temperature. Store leftovers in the refrigerator for up to 4 days, or freeze for up to 3 months.

Garden of Greens Spoonbread

Makes 1 regular loaf or 2 mini loaves
(enough for about 12 regular or 24 small treats)

This greens-packed bread tastes especially good to dogs because of a secret ingredient: beef baby food! Traditional spoonbread is baked in a different kind of pan, but using a loaf pan for this recipe makes it easy to scoop out treat-sized spoonfuls. The edges will be firm, but the middle will be softer.

3 tablespoons canola oil, divided

½ cup nonfat plain yogurt

1 cup cornmeal

2 cups low-sodium chicken or beef broth, or water combined
with ½ teaspoon sea salt

2 (2.5 ounce) jars beef or chicken baby food

2 eggs, lightly beaten

1 cup minced fresh greens (like collards, kale, or mustard greens)

1. Preheat the oven to 400 degrees. Coat a loaf pan with 1 tablespoon of the canola oil, and put the pan in the oven as it preheats.

2. In a small bowl, combine the yogurt with ½ cup ice water.

3. In a large saucepan, stir together the cornmeal and broth or water. Bring to a boil over high heat, then lower the heat and cook, stirring constantly,

for 5 minutes or until the mixture becomes very thick. Remove from the heat and stir in the remaining ingredients in the following order: yogurt mixture, baby food, eggs, the remaining 2 tablespoons canola oil, and the minced greens.

4. Remove the loaf pan from the hot oven and pour the batter into the pan. Immediately return the pan to the oven and bake for 50 minutes, or about 20 minutes for mini loaves—or until the top is deep golden brown. Cool on a rack for 15 minutes, then scoop out servings. Keep in the refrigerator, covered, for up to 2 days, or store frozen treats in a freezer bag for up to 2 months.

Pumpkin Molasses Millet Bread

Makes 1 regular loaf or 2 mini loaves
(enough for about 12 regular or 24 small treats)

This easy recipe is the perfect way to use up the pieces of pumpkin left-over from the jack-o'-lantern carving or a can of pumpkin puree that's been in your cupboard since last November. The bread isn't too sweet, and the addition of ricotta cheese gives it a protein boost.

1 cup whole-wheat pastry flour
1 cup millet flour (or any other whole-grain flour)
1 teaspoon baking soda
1 teaspoon cinnamon
1 cup cooked fresh or canned (unsweetened) pumpkin puree
½ cup part-skim ricotta cheese
½ cup molasses
¼ cup olive oil

1. Preheat the oven to 350 degrees. Spray a loaf pan with cooking spray.

2. In a large bowl, combine the whole-wheat flour, millet flour, baking soda, and cinnamon.

3. In a separate bowl, mix together the pumpkin puree, ricotta cheese, molasses, and olive oil until well combined. Add the pumpkin mixture to the flour mixture and stir until just combined. The batter will be lumpy.

4. Pour the batter into the prepared loaf pan and bake for 1 hour, or about 30 minutes for mini loaves—or until a toothpick inserted into the middle comes out clean.

5. Cool the loaf on a rack for 15 minutes, then remove from the pan. Slice and serve warm or at room temperature. Store leftovers in the refrigerator for up to 3 days, or freeze for up to 2 months.

Salmon-'n'-Ginger Soy Bread

Makes 1 regular loaf or 2 mini loaves
(enough for about 12 regular or 24 small treats)

Dog treats with an Asian flair? Your shih tzu is going to love these!
Fish and soy combine for a high-protein, low-carb treat.

1 cup soy flour
1 cup brown rice flour
2 teaspoons baking soda
1 cup nonfat plain yogurt
2 tablespoons peanut oil
1 tablespoon low-sodium soy sauce
1 tablespoon grated fresh ginger, or 1 teaspoon ground
1 cup cooked fresh or canned, drained flaked salmon
1 tablespoon sesame seeds

1. Preheat the oven to 325 degrees. Spray the loaf pan with cooking spray.

2. In a large bowl, combine the soy flour, brown rice flour, and baking soda. Mix well.

3. In a separate bowl, combine the yogurt, peanut oil, soy sauce, and ginger. Mix well. Add the yogurt mixture to the flour mixture and stir just until combined. Fold in the salmon.

4. Pour the batter into the loaf pan. Sprinkle the top with the sesame seeds. Bake for 1 hour, or about 30 minutes for mini loaves—or until a toothpick inserted into the middle comes out clean.

5. Cool the loaf on a rack for 15 minutes, then remove from the pan. Slice and serve warm or at room temperature. Store leftovers in the refrigerator for up to 2 days, or freeze for up to 1 month.

CHAPTER SIX

Bow-Wow Biscuits and Scones

~

A lot of dog treats are called biscuits, *which is also the British word for* cookie. *But I think of biscuits as those fluffy round breakfast concoctions so beloved in the South, and that's what I mean by biscuits in this chapter. Biscuits and scones are similar—scone being the British incarnation—but for the purposes of this book, I use* biscuits *to describe flaky morsels that are rolled and cut out, and* scones *to describe those that are dropped from a spoon onto a baking sheet. In fact, if you don't have the patience for rolling out the biscuits (I know the feeling!), you can always drop them on the baking sheet, scone-style, regardless of the recipe, although you may need to increase the liquid slightly to make them more "drop-able." Similarly, you can slightly decrease the liquid in any scone recipe to make it more amenable to rolling and cutting out.*

Biscuits and scones make great dog treats because you can make them any size— larger for big dogs, smaller for the little guys. For biscuits, use a regular (about 2½-inch round) biscuit cutter, or use a mini (about 1-inch round) biscuit cutter to make small biscuits. If you don't have a biscuit cutter, the top of a wine glass works for cutting out regular biscuits, and an inverted shot glass will make neat little mini biscuits.

Sweet Potato Surprise Biscuits

Makes about 18 regular or 36 small biscuits

These rich orange biscuits are filled with nutrient-dense sweet potatoes and taste delicious to most dogs. For flakier results, keep the butter in the refrigerator until the last minute. If you don't want to use any animal products in this recipe, you can substitute shortening or margarine for the butter, but look for the non-hydrogenated kind, that says it contains no trans fats. You can usually find this variety in health food stores, and in an increasing number of regular grocery stores.

2 cups whole-wheat pastry flour

1 tablespoon baking powder

¼ teaspoon cinnamon

¼ cup unsalted butter

1 cup mashed sweet potatoes

¼ cup molasses

½ cup unsweetened soy milk or water, plus more as needed

1. Preheat the oven to 400 degrees.

2. In a large bowl, combine the flour, baking powder, and cinnamon. Cut in the butter with a fork or pastry blender until the mixture resembles coarse crumbs. (You can also combine in a food processor, using short pulses.)

3. In a separate bowl, combine the mashed sweet potatoes and molasses. Fold the sweet potato mixture into the flour mixture, then add the soy milk or water, one tablespoon at a time, until the dough is just moist enough to form a ball.

4. Turn the dough onto a lightly floured surface and knead for about 10 seconds. Roll the dough to about a ½-inch thickness and cut out rounds with a biscuit cutter dipped in flour, or form the dough into balls with your hands and flatten them slightly.

5. Transfer the biscuits to an ungreased baking sheet. Bake the biscuits for 12 minutes, or 8 minutes for small biscuits—or until they turn a deep golden brown. Remove the baking sheet from the oven and allow the biscuits to cool for 15 minutes before serving. Serve warm or at room temperature. Store leftovers in an airtight container in the refrigerator for up to 3 days, or in the freezer for up to 2 months.

Beef Stew Biscuits

Makes about 18 biscuits

These biscuits look plain, but surprise! Inside, they have a rich, meaty filling. Baking them in a cake pan makes them like pull-apart rolls.

¾ cup shredded or minced cooked beef

1 tablespoon cooked peas, mashed with a fork

2 tablespoons mashed or minced cooked potatoes

2 tablespoons cooked carrots, mashed with a fork

2 cups whole-wheat pastry flour

1 tablespoon baking powder

½ to ¾ cup low-sodium beef or chicken broth

¼ cup canola oil

1 tablespoon dried oregano

1. Preheat the oven to 375 degrees. Spray a 13 x 9–inch cake pan or casserole dish with cooking spray.

2. In a medium-sized bowl, combine the beef, peas, potatoes, and carrots. Mix well with a fork until well combined. Set aside.

3. In a large bowl, combine the flour and baking powder. Add ½ cup of the broth and canola oil. Stir with a fork until combined. If necessary, add more broth, 1 tablespoon at a time, until the mixture sticks together and you can form it into a ball. Divide the ball into 18 equal-sized (roughly) pieces.

4. Working with one piece at a time, use your hands to flatten each ball into a 2-inch round. Put approximately 2 teaspoons of the beef mixture in the center of the round and form the dough around the filling, shaping it into a ball. Put the ball into the prepared cake pan. It's OK for them to touch. Repeat with the remaining dough until the pan is filled with the biscuit balls. Sprinkle the tops with the oregano.

5. Bake the biscuits for 15 minutes, or until they turn a deep golden brown. Remove the pan from the oven and allow the biscuits to cool for 15 minutes before serving. Serve warm or at room temperature, pulling the biscuits out of the pan as needed. Store leftovers covered in the refrigerator for up to 2 days, or in the freezer for up to 2 months. (Separate the biscuits before freezing so you can take them out and defrost them one at a time, as needed.)

Double-Butter Biscuits

Makes 18 regular or 36 small biscuits

Contrary to the name, this recipe contains no dairy butter. Instead, these biscuits are rich with peanut butter and sesame butter, sometimes called *tahini*. You can find sesame butter in the health food section of your grocery store, or at a Greek or Middle Eastern specialty store.

2 cups whole-wheat pastry flour
1 tablespoon baking powder
½ teaspoon sea salt
¼ cup natural peanut butter
2 tablespoons sesame butter (*tahini*)
2 tablespoons molasses
½ cup nonfat plain yogurt

1. Preheat the oven to 425 degrees.

2. In a large bowl, combine the flour, baking powder, and salt. Using a fork, stir in the peanut butter, sesame butter, and molasses, mixing until the batter resembles coarse crumbs. (You can also combine in a food processor, using short pulses.) Mix in the yogurt, then gather the dough into a ball.

3. Turn the dough onto a lightly floured surface and roll it to about a ½-inch thickness. Cut out rounds with a biscuit cutter dipped in flour.

4. Transfer the biscuits to an ungreased baking sheet. Bake the biscuits for 12 minutes, or 8 minutes for small biscuits—or until they turn a deep golden brown. Remove the baking sheet from the oven and allow the biscuits to cool for 15 minutes before serving. Serve warm or at room temperature. Store leftovers in an airtight container in the refrigerator for up to 3 days, or in the freezer for up to 2 months.

Cottage Cheese Basil Biscuits

Makes 36 small biscuits

These little nips are full of cheesy goodness, and they're crunchy like the dog treats your dog is probably accustomed to. They are easy and fun to make, and you might want a nibble, too. But be warned: they're addictive.

2 cups whole-wheat pastry flour

½ teaspoon sea salt

I tablespoon baking powder

2 tablespoons fresh minced basil leaves

I cup grated Parmesan or Romano cheese

⅓ cup olive oil

I cup low-fat cottage cheese

I egg

I tablespoon low-sodium chicken broth (optional)

1. Preheat the oven to 400 degrees.

2. In a large bowl, combine the flour, salt, baking powder, and 1 tablespoon of the basil. Mix to combine.

3. In a small bowl, mix the remaining tablespoon of basil and ½ cup of Parmesan or Romano cheese. Set aside.

4. In a separate bowl, mix together the olive oil, cottage cheese, and the remaining ½ cup Parmesan or Romano cheese until well combined. Add the cottage cheese mixture to the flour mixture and stir until the ingredients are well incorporated. If the dough seems very dry, add a little water, 1 tablespoon at a time, until you can form the dough into small balls with your hands.

5. Pull off a small piece of dough and form it into a 1-inch ball, then flatten it with your palms so it is about ¼-inch thick or even thinner. Repeat with the remaining dough. (You can also roll this dough out and cut it as you would for other biscuits, but use a small cutter.) Place the disks about 1 inch apart on an ungreased baking sheet. You will have enough dough to fill more than one baking sheet.

6. Beat the egg with the chicken broth or 1 tablespoon of water. Brush the top of each biscuit with the thinned egg, then sprinkle with the basil-cheese mixture. Bake the biscuits for 10 minutes, or until they turn golden brown. Remove the baking sheet from the oven and allow the biscuits to cool for 15 minutes before serving. Store leftovers in an airtight container in the refrigerator for up to 3 days, or in the freezer for up to 3 months.

Parmesan Chicken Scones

Makes about 18 regular or 36 small scones

If you have just a little bit of leftover chicken, these savory scones will put it to good use.

2 cups whole-wheat pastry flour
½ cup grated Parmesan cheese
1 tablespoon baking powder
1 teaspoon baking soda
1 teaspoon dried oregano
1 cup nonfat plain yogurt
1 egg, lightly beaten
½ cup canola oil
½ cup minced cooked chicken

1. Preheat the oven to 400 degrees.

2. In a large bowl, combine the flour, ¼ cup of the Parmesan cheese, the baking powder, baking soda, and oregano.

3. In a separate bowl, combine the yogurt, egg, and canola oil. Add the yogurt mixture to the flour mixture and stir until well combined. Fold in the chicken.

4. Drop the batter into 18 regular or 36 small scones, about 1 inch apart, on 2 ungreased baking sheets (or bake them in two batches). Sprinkle the scones with the remaining ¼ cup of Parmesan cheese and bake for 12 minutes, or 8 minutes for small biscuits—or until the scones turn golden brown.

5. Remove the pans from the oven and allow to cool for 10 minutes before serving. Serve warm or at room temperature. Store leftovers in an airtight container in the refrigerator for up to 3 days, or in the freezer for up to 2 months.

Tuna Yogurt Scones

Makes about 18 regular or 36 small scones

Tuna and yogurt give these scones a tangy, fishy flavor dogs can't resist.

2 cups whole-wheat pastry flour
1 tablespoon baking powder
1 cup nonfat plain yogurt
1 egg, lightly beaten
3 ounces cooked fresh or canned, drained flaked tuna

1. Preheat the oven to 400 degrees.

2. In a large bowl, combine the flour and baking powder.

3. In a separate bowl, combine the yogurt and the egg. Add the yogurt mixture to the flour mixture and stir with a fork until just combined. The batter will be lumpy. Stir in the tuna and mix until well combined.

4. Drop the batter by tablespoons or teaspoons (depending on what size you want the scones to be) about 1 inch apart on an ungreased cookie sheet (you may need to bake in two or more batches). Bake the scones for 15 minutes, or 10 minutes for small scones—or until they turn golden brown.

5. Remove the pan from the oven and allow to cool for 10 minutes before serving. Serve warm or at room temperature. Store leftovers in an airtight container in the refrigerator for up to 2 days, or in the freezer for up to 2 months.

Seaweed Scones

Makes about 18 regular or 36 small scones

Filled with healthy micronutrients, seaweed is an often-overlooked source of good nutrition for both pets and people. Sure, it looks weird, but it tastes delicious, especially when it's slipped into a scone. For this recipe, you can soak dried seaweed from the health food store or Asian grocery, or you can use your own leftover seaweed salad from a trip to the sushi bar. If you use leftover seaweed salad, ignore the soaking step and don't add the vinegar and soy sauce, but do chop it into very small pieces before adding it to the dough.

Because this recipe uses brown rice flour, which doesn't contain gluten, it won't hold together the same way wheat flour scones will. Xanthan gum can help, but it isn't absolutely necessary, especially since your dog won't mind an extra crumbly scone.

½ ounce dried wakame seaweed, whole or cut, or leftover seaweed salad

1 tablespoon rice vinegar (if using dried seaweed)

1 teaspoon soy sauce (if using dried seaweed)

2 cups brown rice flour

1 tablespoon baking powder

1 teaspoon xanthan gum (optional)

½ cup plain (unsweetened) soy milk, plus more as needed

1 egg, lightly beaten

1. Preheat the oven to 400 degrees.

2. If using dried seaweed, in a medium bowl, cover the seaweed with warm water and let it soak for 5 minutes. Drain and squeeze out the excess water, then mince the seaweed. Add the rice vinegar and soy sauce, and stir to coat. If using seaweed salad, mince the seaweed.

3. In a large bowl, combine the flour, baking powder, and xanthan gum (if using).

4. In a separate bowl, combine the soy milk and egg. Add the soy milk mixture to the flour mixture and stir until combined. Stir in the seaweed mixture. The dough should be pretty stiff. If it is too dry to form into balls, add a little more soy milk, a tablespoon at a time. If the mixture is too wet, add a little more rice flour.

5. Drop the batter by tablespoons or teaspoons (depending on what size you want the scones to be) about 1 inch apart on an ungreased baking sheet (you may need to bake in two or more batches). Bake the scones for 15 minutes, or 10 minutes for small scones—or until they turn golden brown.

6. Remove the pan from the oven and allow to cool for 10 minutes before serving. Serve warm or at room temperature. Store leftovers in an airtight container in the refrigerator for up to 2 days, or in the freezer for up to 2 months.

{CHAPTER SEVEN}

Doggie Bar Cookies

~

I love making bar cookies for dog treats because you can cut them to any size you need. Plus, I get impatient with rolling and cutting out cookies or dropping them onto baking sheet after baking sheet. With bar cookies, you can just whip up the dough, spread it in the pan, and bake.

These recipes are all designed to fit into a 13 x 9–inch baking pan, with the exception of the biscotti, which is shaped into a loaf. However, you can reduce any of these recipes by half and bake them in an 8-inch square baking pan if you don't want to make as much.

Beefy Barley Bars

Makes about 16 large or 32 small treats

These meaty treats taste great with beef, but feel free to substitute lamb, chicken, turkey, or even venison.

2 cups barley flour

1 teaspoon baking powder

¼ teaspoon baking soda

½ cup canola oil

½ cup unsweetened applesauce

2 tablespoons molasses

2 eggs, lightly beaten

2 cups cooked shredded, minced, or ground beef

1. Preheat the oven to 375 degrees. Spray a 13 x 9–inch baking pan with cooking spray.

2. In a medium-sized bowl, combine the flour, baking powder, and baking soda.

3. In a separate bowl, combine the canola oil, applesauce, molasses, and eggs. Add the oil mixture to the flour mixture and stir until well incorporated. Fold in the beef.

4. Pour the batter into the baking pan and spread it to cover the bottom evenly. Bake for 20 minutes, or until the top turns golden brown and the middle doesn't quiver when you gently shake the pan. Remove the pan from the oven and cool on a rack for 10 minutes. Score the bars into the size you want, and cool for an additional 30 minutes to 1 hour. Serve the bars warm or at room temperature. Store in an airtight container in the refrigerator for up to 2 days, or in the freezer for up to 2 months.

Carrot Cornmeal Bars

Makes about 16 large or 32 small treats

Cornmeal gives these cookies crunch, and carrots give them both an extra dose of nutrients and a beautiful color.

½ cup canola oil

½ cup unsweetened applesauce

¼ cup honey

2 eggs

1 cup cornmeal

1 teaspoon baking powder

¼ teaspoon salt

2 cups shredded carrots

1. Preheat the oven to 350 degrees. Spray a 13 x 9–inch baking pan with cooking spray.

2. In a medium-sized bowl, combine the canola oil, applesauce, honey, and eggs. Beat until well combined.

3. In a separate bowl, stir together the cornmeal, baking powder, and salt. Add the cornmeal mixture to the oil mixture and stir to combine. Fold in the carrots.

4. Pour the batter into the baking pan and spread it to cover the bottom evenly. Bake for 30 minutes, or until the top turns golden brown and the middle doesn't quiver when you gently shake the pan. Remove the pan from the oven and cool on a rack for 10 minutes. Score the bars into the size you want, and cool for an additional 30 minutes to 1 hour. Cut the bars and serve warm or at room temperature. Store in an airtight container in the refrigerator for up to 3 days, or in the freezer for up to 3 months.

Brown Rice Biscotti

Makes about 16 large or 32 small treats

This recipe looks like a lot of work because you have to bake it twice, but the results will be well worth the effort. Just ask your dog. You can use all brown rice flour in this recipe, but if you do, bake it in a loaf pan so it doesn't spread too much, and/or add a teaspoon of xanthan gum to help hold it together.

1 cup brown rice flour
1 cup whole-wheat pastry flour
1 tablespoon baking powder
1 tablespoon anise or fennel seeds
4 eggs
½ cup canola oil
½ cup cooked brown rice

1. Preheat the oven to 375 degrees. Spray a 13 x 9–inch baking pan with cooking spray.

2. In a medium-sized bowl, combine the brown rice flour, whole-wheat flour, baking powder, and anise or fennel seeds.

3. In a small bowl, separate 1 egg and combine the yolk with 1 tablespoon of water. Set aside. Reserve the white for another use.

4. In a medium-sized bowl, beat together the separated egg white and the remaining 3 eggs. Stir in the canola oil and ½ cup water. Add the flour mixture to the egg mixture and stir to combine, then fold in the brown rice.

5. Turn the batter onto the prepared baking pan. Shape it into a long, thin, rounded loaf or rope shape, about 2 inches wide by 12 inches long. Flatten the top slightly. Brush with the yolk/water mixture. Bake for 30 minutes, or until the top turns deep golden brown.

6. Remove the pan from the oven and let the loaf cool for about 10 minutes, then use a serrated knife to carefully slice the loaf into 1-inch slices cut on the diagonal. Arrange the slices cut-side down on the baking sheet and return it to the oven. Bake for 10 more minutes, or until the bars are crisp and golden. Let the bars cool for about an hour and serve at room temperature. Store in an airtight container in the refrigerator for up to 1 week, or in the freezer up to 6 months.

Chicken Fingers

Makes about 16 large or 32 small treats

These tasty cookie-like strips are filled with chicken rather than sugar. What dog could resist?

1½ cups whole-wheat pastry flour

¾ cup soy flour

2 teaspoons garlic powder

1 teaspoon dried oregano

1 teaspoon dried basil

1 teaspoon baking soda

½ cup canola oil

¾ cup unsweetened applesauce

½ cup molasses

2 eggs

2 cups shredded or minced cooked chicken

1. Preheat the oven to 375 degrees. Spray a 13 x 9–inch baking pan with cooking spray.

2. In a large mixing bowl, stir together the whole-wheat flour, soy flour, garlic powder, oregano, basil, and baking soda.

3. In a separate bowl, combine the canola oil, applesauce, and molasses. Add the oil mixture to the flour mixture and beat with an electric mixer on medium speed for 1 minute. Add the eggs, one at a time, beating well after each addition. Stir in the chicken.

4. Pour the batter into the prepared baking pan. Bake for 20 minutes, or until the edges turn golden brown and just begin to pull away from the sides of the pan. Remove the pan from the oven and cool on a rack for 10 minutes. Score the bars into strips of your desired size, and allow to cool completely before cutting the cookies along the score lines. Store the leftovers in an airtight container in the refrigerator for up to 2 days, or in the freezer for up to 2 months.

Peanut Butter Flax Bars

Makes about 16 large or 32 small treats

Ground flaxseeds have omega-3 fatty acids that can help dogs maintain a healthy skin and coat. Flax is good for *you*, too, so you might consider giving these treats a nibble.

1 cup ground flaxseeds

2 cups rolled oats

1 tablespoon baking soda

1 cup canola oil

1 cup natural peanut butter

4 eggs

1. Preheat the oven to 350 degrees. Spray a 13 x 9–inch baking pan with cooking spray.

2. Combine the flaxseeds, oats, and baking soda in a large mixing bowl. Add the canola oil, peanut butter, and eggs. Beat with an electric mixer on medium speed for 2 minutes.

3. Press the dough into the baking pan and bake for 15 minutes, or until the bars turn golden brown. Remove the pan from the oven and cool the bars on a wire rack for 10 minutes. Score into 16 or 32 bars. Allow the cookies to cool completely, then cut along the score lines. Store leftovers in an airtight container in the refrigerator for up to 4 days, or in the freezer for up to 4 months.

Great Barrier Reef Bars

Makes about 16 large or 32 small treats

These bars are deliciously fishy—at least, that's what dogs think! These are great skin-and-coat-conditioning treats because of the fish and the flax.

I cup ground flaxseeds

I cup cornmeal

½ cup unsalted butter, softened

½ teaspoon salt

2 cups flaked cooked fish (such as salmon, tuna, or cod)

2 eggs, lightly beaten

¼ cup mayonnaise

¼ cup nonfat plain yogurt

½ teaspoon garlic powder

2 tablespoons grated Parmesan cheese

1. Preheat the oven to 350 degrees. Spray a 13 x 9–inch baking pan with cooking spray.

2. In a large bowl or the bowl of a food processor, combine the flaxseeds, cornmeal, butter, and salt. Mix or process until the mixture resembles coarse crumbs. Press the mixture into the bottom of the prepared baking pan.

3. In the same bowl (now emptied but you don't need to clean it), combine the fish, eggs, mayonnaise, yogurt, and garlic powder. Stir to combine. Spread the fish mixture over the crumb mixture. Sprinkle with the Parmesan cheese.

4. Bake for 30 minutes, or until the topping sizzles and turns golden brown. Remove from the oven and cool completely. Cut the cookies into the desired size. Serve at room temperature or chilled. Store in an airtight container in the refrigerator for up to 2 days, or in the freezer for up to 2 months.

CHAPTER EIGHT

Terrific Turnovers

~

*Because they hide a surprise filling, turnovers are fun to eat.
Will your dog think so? Why not try a batch and find out?
They're fun to make, too. All of the turnover recipes in this chapter begin
with a pastry sheet that is cut into pieces, filled, folded,
and baked. It would be nice and easy if premade whole-grain
pastry sheets were widely available in grocery stores,
but since I've only ever seen prepared pastry sheets made with
white flour (not a healthful choice for dogs),
the recipes in this chapter require a homemade sheet of
Puppy Pastry Dough (page 80) as their base. Mix up a batch of this
pooch-friendly pastry and then proceed with the filling recipes
that follow in this chapter. After a few batches, you'll be able to start
inventing your own fillings. (Just remember to use
dog-safe ingredients only.)*

Puppy Pastry Dough

Makes enough dough for 18 regular or 36 small turnovers

This dough is your go-to recipe whenever you want to fill a dog treat with a yummy filling. Be sure to use whole-wheat flour for this dough, because other flours won't have enough gluten to hold the turnovers together. Even with whole-wheat flour, you'll need to handle the dough carefully so you don't break it. Don't roll it so thin that you can't pick it up without it falling apart, and use lots of flour on your rolling surface.

1 tablespoon ground flaxseeds

1½ cups whole-wheat pastry flour

¼ cup soy flour

1 teaspoon salt

3 tablespoons canola oil

¼ cup soy milk

1. In a small bowl, stir the flaxseeds into ¼ cup water and allow the mixture to sit for 10 minutes.

2. Combine the whole-wheat flour, soy flour, salt, and canola oil in a large bowl. Mix with a fork, breaking up the chunks, until all ingredients are well combined.

3. Stir the soy milk into to the flaxseed mixture, then drizzle it over the flour mixture a little at a time, tossing with a fork as you go. When the dough begins to get too moist to toss, work it with your hands, incorporating all the ingredients. Form the dough into a ball with your hands. If it is too sticky, add a little more wheat flour. If it is too dry and crumbly, add a little more water. When dough reaches the desired consistency, proceed with one of the following recipes in this chapter.

You can also make this dough up to two days before you plan on using it. Wrap it in a wet paper towel and seal it in an airtight container. Keep it in the refrigerator until ready to use. You might need to bring the dough to room temperature to facilitate rolling it out without crumbling. If it's dry, knead in a little more oil.

Chicken Apple Turnovers

Makes 18 regular or 36 small turnovers

These sweet-and-savory turnovers are full of protein and fiber.

¾ cup minced cooked chicken

½ cup peeled minced fresh apple

¼ cup nonfat plain yogurt

¼ teaspoon garlic powder

¼ teaspoon ground cumin

1 batch Puppy Pastry Dough (page 80)

1. Preheat the oven to 350 degrees. Spray 2 baking sheets with cooking spray.

2. In a medium-sized bowl, combine the chicken, apple, yogurt, garlic powder, and cumin. Mix thoroughly.

3. Divide the pastry dough in half. On a well-floured surface, roll out half the dough to ¼-inch thickness. Carefully cut it into 9 large or 18 small circles or rectangles (depending on the size of the treats you prefer to make). For larger treats, put about 2 tablespoons of the chicken mixture onto each piece of dough; for smaller treats, about 1 tablespoon. Using a brush or your fingers, moisten the edges of each turnover, then carefully fold the dough over the filling. Press the edges with your fingers to seal, then crimp with a fork. Repeat with the other half of the dough.

4. Using a spatula, carefully transfer the turnovers to the prepared baking sheets. Bake for 20 minutes, or 10 minutes for small turnovers—or until golden brown. Allow the turnovers to cool on a rack for at least 30 minutes before serving—that filling inside can be hot, and you don't want anybody to burn a tongue! When the turnovers have cooled completely, store them in an airtight container in the refrigerator for up to 2 days, or freeze them for up to 2 months.

Steak-and-Egg Surprise

Makes 18 regular or 36 small turnovers

This recipe makes a yummy breakfast treat for your dog, and it's a good way to avoid wasting the last few pieces of steak or the scrambled eggs leftover from your own breakfast.

½ cup minced cooked steak
½ cup chopped scrambled, fried, or boiled eggs
1 tablespoon grated Parmesan cheese
1 tablespoon mayonnaise
1 batch Puppy Pastry Dough (page 80)

1. Preheat the oven to 350 degrees. Spray 2 baking sheets with cooking spray.

2. In a medium-sized bowl, combine the steak, eggs, Parmesan cheese, and mayonnaise. Mix thoroughly.

3. Divide the pastry dough in half. On a well-floured surface, roll out half the dough to a ¼-inch thickness. Carefully cut it into 9 large or 18 small circles or rectangles (depending on the size of the treats you prefer to make). For larger treats, put about 2 tablespoons of the steak mixture onto each piece of dough; for smaller treats, about 1 tablespoon. Using a brush or your fingers, moisten the edges of each turnover, then carefully fold the dough over the filling. Press the edges with your fingers to seal, then crimp with a fork. Repeat with the other half of the dough.

4. Using a spatula, carefully transfer the turnovers to the prepared baking sheets. Bake for 20 minutes, or 10 minutes for small turnovers—or until golden brown. Allow the turnovers to cool on a rack for at least 30 minutes before serving—that filling inside can be hot, and you don't want anybody to burn a tongue! When the turnovers have cooled completely, store them in an airtight container in the refrigerator for up to 2 days, or freeze them for up to 2 months.

Turkey Liver Turnovers

Makes 18 regular or 36 small turnovers

Don't throw away the valuable turkey liver from the Thanksgiving turkey, or from any other turkey you cook during the year. You can sometimes buy turkey livers from the meat counter, separate from the rest of the turkey. This recipe also tastes good when made with chicken liver, but avoid substituting with beef liver, which contains a lot of toxins.

¾ cup minced cooked turkey livers
¼ cup low-sodium turkey or chicken broth
¼ teaspoon garlic powder
¼ teaspoon sea salt
2 tablespoons mayonnaise
1 batch Puppy Pastry Dough (page 80)

1. Preheat the oven to 350 degrees. Spray 2 baking sheets with cooking spray.

2. In a medium-sized bowl, combine the livers, broth, garlic powder, salt, and mayonnaise. Mix thoroughly.

3. Divide the pastry dough in half. On a well-floured surface, roll out half the dough to a ¼-inch thickness. Carefully cut it into 9 large or 18 small circles or rectangles (depending on the size of the treats you prefer to

make). For larger treats, put about 2 tablespoons of the liver mixture onto each piece of dough; for smaller treats, about 1 tablespoon. Using a brush or your fingers, moisten the edges of each turnover, then carefully fold the dough over the filling. Press the edges with your fingers to seal, then crimp with a fork. Repeat with the other half of the dough.

4. Using a spatula, carefully transfer the turnovers to the prepared baking sheets. Bake for 20 minutes, or 10 minutes for small turnovers—or until golden brown. Allow the turnovers to cool on a rack for at least 30 minutes before serving—that filling inside can be hot, and you don't want anybody to burn a tongue! When the turnovers have cooled completely, store them in an airtight container in the refrigerator for up to 2 days, or freeze them for up to 2 months.

Full-o-Fishes Knishes

Makes 18 regular or 36 small turnovers

Knishes are a kind of turnover or dumpling common in Eastern Europe and popular in Jewish culture. Many traditional versions contain mashed potatoes, buckwheat, ground meat, or liver (as in the recipe for Turkey Liver Turnovers (page 85), which is arguably even more knish-like than this one). This omega-3–rich version has a fresh fishy taste your dog will love.

You can use any kind of fish in this recipe—salmon, tuna, cod, or whatever else you have leftover. However, avoid using shellfish. If we're going to name this recipe for a Jewish treat, we'd best keep it kosher.

¾ cup minced cooked fish

2 tablespoons heavy cream or nonfat plain yogurt

½ teaspoon dried dill weed

¼ teaspoon paprika

¼ teaspoon sea salt

1 batch Puppy Pastry Dough (page 80)

1. Preheat the oven to 350 degrees. Spray 2 baking sheets with cooking spray.

2. In a medium-sized bowl, combine the fish, cream or yogurt, dill weed, paprika, and salt. Mix thoroughly.

3. Divide the pastry dough in half. On a well-floured surface, roll out half the dough to a ¼-inch thickness. Carefully cut it into 9 large or 18 small circles or rectangles (depending on the size of the treats you prefer to make). For larger treats, put about 2 tablespoons of the fish mixture onto each piece of dough; for smaller treats, about 1 tablespoon. Using a brush or your fingers, moisten the edges of each turnover, then carefully fold the dough over the filling. Press the edges with your fingers to seal, then crimp with a fork. Repeat with the other half of the dough.

4. Using a spatula, carefully transfer the turnovers to the prepared baking sheets. Bake for 20 minutes, or 10 minutes for small turnovers—or until golden brown. Allow the turnovers to cool on a rack for at least 30 minutes before serving—that filling inside can be hot, and you don't want anybody to burn a tongue! When the turnovers have cooled completely, store them in an airtight container in the refrigerator for up to 2 days, or freeze them for up to 2 months.

Hamburger
Sweet Potato Pockets

Makes 18 regular or 36 small turnovers

These savory little envelopes of burger and sweet potato make pretty and surprising treats for both pets and people. The combination of ground beef and sweet potato may sound strange, but try it. It's unexpectedly delicious.

For that small group of vegetarian dogs, you can also make this recipe with black beans instead of ground beef. Drain and rinse all the salt and goo from about ¾ cup canned black beans. Mash them well with a fork, and substitute them for the meat.

½ cup cooked ground beef, thoroughly crumbled

½ cup mashed sweet potatoes

1 egg, lightly beaten

½ teaspoon ground cumin

½ teaspoon sea salt

¼ teaspoon cinnamon

1 batch Puppy Pastry Dough (page 80)

1. Preheat the oven to 350 degrees. Spray 2 baking sheets with cooking spray.

2. In a medium-sized bowl, combine the ground beef, sweet potatoes, egg, cumin, salt, and cinnamon. Mix thoroughly.

3. Divide the pastry dough in half. On a well-floured surface, roll out half the dough to a ¼-inch thickness. Carefully cut it into 9 large or 18 small circles or rectangles (depending on the size of the treats you prefer to make). For larger treats, put about 2 tablespoons of the beef mixture onto each piece of dough; for smaller treats, about 1 tablespoon. Using a brush or your fingers, moisten the edges of each turnover, then carefully fold the dough over the filling. Press the edges with your fingers to seal, then crimp with a fork. Repeat with the other half of the dough.

4. Using a spatula, carefully transfer the turnovers to the prepared baking sheets. Bake for 20 minutes, or 10 minutes for small turnovers—or until golden brown. Allow the turnovers to cool on a rack for at least 30 minutes before serving—that filling inside can be hot, and you don't want anybody to burn a tongue! When the turnovers have cooled completely, store them in an airtight container in the refrigerator for up to 2 days, or freeze them for up to 2 months.

{CHAPTER NINE}

Real Dogs Eat Quiche

~

Quiche makes a fantastic dog treat because eggs are
one of the most complete sources of protein, and the dog-friendly
ingredients you add to the egg mixture make the quiche more fun.
Plus, quiche is incredibly easy to make.

Typically, quiche is baked in a crust, but it doesn't have to be.
Since quiches bake beautifully without a crust, and
since this book already has a whole chapter on pies with crusts,
all the quiches in this chapter are crust-free. Dogs don't need
to be eating a lot of crust anyway.

Quiches are flexible, so make yours in whatever way
you think sounds most fun and convenient for you and your dog.
I give directions for making each quiche in a pie plate.
However, you can adapt any recipe in this chapter by
baking them in a twelve-cup or two six-cup muffin tins, or in
two twelve-cup mini muffin tins. They should all work out
about right, but bake quiches in a muffin tin for about
half the time indicated, and about a quarter of the time
for mini muffins—or until the egg is set.

Quiche Lassie

Makes 12 regular or 24 small treats

You've probably heard of Quiche Lorraine. Well, who the heck is Lorraine? We're more interested in Lassie, and this quiche is designed for her (as a reward for rescuing Timmy from that well). I don't usually recommend giving dogs cured meats because of all the sodium and curing chemicals, but a little bit of low-sodium ham gives this quiche a great flavor. The more natural the ham, the better.

4 eggs
1 cup nonfat plain yogurt
½ cup finely chopped low-sodium ham
½ cup shredded Gruyère cheese

1. Preheat the oven to 375 degrees. Spray a 9-inch pie plate with cooking spray.
2. In a large bowl, beat the eggs, then beat in the yogurt.
3. Pour the egg mixture into the pie plate. Sprinkle it with the ham, followed by the cheese. Bake the quiche for 40 minutes, or until the quiche turns golden and looks cooked in the middle (gently shake the pie plate—the middle shouldn't wiggle).

4. Remove the quiche from the oven and cool completely on a wire rack. Slice and serve. Store leftovers in an airtight container in the refrigerator for up to 2 days, or freeze individual slices for up to 2 months.

Green Dog Quiche

Makes 12 regular or 24 small treats

This brightly colored quiche, packed with antioxidants, is earth-friendly as well as nutritious if you make it with free-range eggs and organic vegetables. Although the eggs make it protein-rich, if you prefer, you can up the ante by adding a cup of chopped chicken, turkey, or fish.

4 eggs

1 cup nonfat plain yogurt

1 tablespoon anise or fennel seeds

½ teaspoon sea salt

½ cup packed finely minced fresh greens (like collards, kale, or mustard greens)

½ cup cooked butternut or acorn squash, finely chopped or mashed

1. Preheat the oven to 350 degrees. Spray a 9-inch pie plate with cooking spray.

2. In a large bowl, beat the eggs, then beat in the yogurt, anise or fennel seeds, and salt. Stir in the greens and squash.

3. Pour the egg mixture into the pie plate. Bake the quiche for 45 minutes, or until the quiche turns golden and looks cooked in the middle (gently shake the pie plate—the middle shouldn't wiggle).

4. Remove the quiche from the oven and cool completely on a wire rack. Slice and serve. Store leftovers in an airtight container in the refrigerator for up to 2 days, or freeze individual slices for up to 2 months.

Creamy Salmon Quiche

Makes 12 regular or 24 small treats

This quiche is a great way to use up that last salmon fillet nobody wanted at dinner last night.

4 eggs
1 cup low-fat cottage cheese
1 cup flaked cooked salmon
2 tablespoons minced fresh parsley

1. Preheat the oven to 350 degrees. Spray a 9-inch pie plate with cooking spray.

2. In a large bowl, beat the eggs, then add the cottage cheese, salmon, and parsley. Stir until well combined.

3. Pour the egg mixture into the pie plate. Bake the quiche for 35 minutes, or until the quiche turns golden and looks cooked in the middle (gently shake the pie plate—the middle shouldn't wiggle).

4. Remove the quiche from the oven and cool completely on a wire rack. Slice and serve. Store leftovers in an airtight container in the refrigerator for up to 2 days, or freeze individual slices for up to 2 months.

Tuna Noodle Casserole Quiche

Makes 12 regular or 24 small treats

This quiche incorporates cooked noodles into the eggs to create an interesting combination of textures. Use leftover egg noodles, spaghetti, macaroni, or any other pasta cut into small pieces. It's canine comfort food!

4 eggs
½ cup nonfat plain yogurt
½ teaspoon sea salt (omit if using canned tuna)
½ cup flaked fresh or canned, drained tuna
½ cup chopped cooked pasta
½ cup packed shredded fresh carrots
¼ cup finely chopped fresh broccoli
¼ cup cooked peas, mashed
1 tablespoon Parmesan cheese

1. Preheat the oven to 350 degrees. Spray a 9-inch pie plate with cooking spray.

2. In a large bowl, beat the eggs, then beat in the yogurt and salt (if using). Stir in the tuna, pasta, carrots, broccoli, and peas.

3. Pour the egg mixture into the pie plate. Sprinkle with Parmesan cheese. Bake the quiche for 45 minutes, or until the quiche turns golden and looks cooked in the middle (gently shake the pie plate—the middle shouldn't wiggle).

4. Remove the quiche from the oven and cool completely on a wire rack. Slice and serve. Store leftovers in an airtight container in the refrigerator for up to 2 days, or freeze individual slices for up to 2 months.

Pork Pie Quiche

Makes 12 regular or 24 small treats

This recipe transforms the traditionally heavy, rich, crust-dominated British pork pie into a quiche. Leftovers from pork chops work well for this recipe. Avoid using cured pork, like sausage, or pork covered in sauce, like barbecued ribs.

4 eggs

½ cup nonfat plain yogurt

1 teaspoon dried sage

½ teaspoon dried thyme

½ teaspoon garlic powder

½ teaspoon sea salt

1 cup minced cooked pork

½ cup leftover mashed potatoes or boiled potatoes mashed with a fork

1. Preheat the oven to 375 degrees. Spray a 9-inch pie plate with cooking spray.
2. In a large bowl, beat the eggs, then beat in the yogurt, sage, thyme, garlic powder, and salt. Stir in the pork and potatoes and mix with a fork until well combined.

3. Spread the mixture evenly into the pie plate. Bake the quiche for 35 minutes, or until the quiche turns golden and looks cooked in the middle (gently shake the pie plate—the middle shouldn't wiggle).

4. Remove from the oven and cool completely on a wire rack. Slice and serve. Store leftovers in an airtight container in the refrigerator for up to 2 days, or freeze individual slices for up to 2 months.

Bacon Cheeseburger Quiche

Makes 12 regular or 24 small treats

This yummy treat may sound like junk food, but fear not. Lean beef, just a little cheese, and low-sodium turkey bacon make this a dog-friendly and nutritious snack that is high in protein.

4 eggs

¼ cup mayonnaise

½ cup nonfat plain yogurt

½ teaspoon garlic powder

1 cup cooked lean ground beef, broken up

2 strips cooked low-sodium turkey bacon, minced

¼ cup finely shredded Cheddar cheese

1. Preheat the oven to 350 degrees. Spray a 9-inch pie plate with cooking spray.

2. In a large bowl, beat the eggs, then beat in the mayonnaise, yogurt, and garlic powder. Stir in the ground beef and pour the mixture into the pie plate. Sprinkle with the bacon, then with the cheese.

3. Bake the quiche for 45 minutes, or until the quiche turns golden and looks cooked in the middle (gently shake the pie plate—the middle shouldn't wiggle).

4. Remove the quiche from the oven and cool completely on a wire rack. Slice and serve. Store leftovers in an airtight container in the refrigerator for up to 2 days, or freeze individual slices for up to 2 months.

Turkey Berry Quiche

Makes 12 regular or 24 small treats

You can use cranberries or blueberries in this recipe, depending on what you have on hand. Either way, chop up the berries well, or process them for a few pulses in a food processor so they are easy to digest. You don't need to cook them first.

4 eggs

¾ cup low-sodium turkey or chicken broth

1 cup minced cooked turkey

½ cup chopped blueberries or cranberries

2 tablespoons corn bread stuffing mix or dried whole-grain bread crumbs

1. Preheat the oven to 350 degrees. Spray a 9-inch pie plate with cooking spray.

2. In a large bowl, beat the eggs with the broth. Stir in the turkey and the berries.

3. Pour the mixture into the pie plate. Sprinkle with the stuffing mix or bread crumbs. Bake the quiche for 45 minutes, or until the quiche turns golden and looks cooked in the middle (gently shake the pie plate—the middle shouldn't wiggle).

4. Remove the quiche from the oven and cool completely on a wire rack. Slice and serve. Store leftovers in an airtight container in the refrigerator for up to 2 days, or freeze individual slices for up to 2 months.

CHAPTER TEN

Grain-Free Goodness

~

*Although dogs are not as strictly carnivorous as cats,
some dogs have developed allergies to grain.
Whether the culprit is too much grain in commercial pet foods,
I don't know. I do know, however, that many pet owners
report softer coats, healthier skin, and glowing health in their dogs
after switching them to a grain-free diet, even if their dogs
aren't officially allergic to grains.*

*In that grain-free spirit, for all the dogs who can't,
shouldn't, or just don't care to eat grains (and for their keepers,
who don't want to feed them grains), the treats in this chapter
are all 100 percent grain-free. Remember, too, that some
of the other recipes in this book are grain-free as well;
all are marked with the grain-free icon.*

Mini Meatballs

Makes about 20 small or 40 tiny meatballs

A lot of meatball recipes contain bread crumbs, but not this one. Who needs 'em? The egg and veggies lighten these meatballs just enough.

½ pound lean ground beef, turkey, or lamb (uncooked)
1 egg, lightly beaten
¼ cup grated carrots
1 tablespoon Parmesan cheese
1 tablespoon low-sodium broth or water

1. Preheat the oven to 350 degrees. Spray a broiler pan or baking pan with cooking spray.

2. In a large bowl, combine the ground meat, egg, carrots, Parmesan cheese, and broth or water, and mix together with your hands until all ingredients are thoroughly incorporated. Shape into about 20 one-inch or about 40 half-inch meatballs.

3. Put the meatballs on the prepared pan. Bake about 35 minutes for one-inch or 25 minutes for half-inch meatballs, or until the meatballs are no longer pink in the middle. Watch that the smaller ones don't burn.

4. Remove the pan from the oven and cool to warm or room temperature before serving. Store leftovers in an airtight container in the refrigerator for up to 2 days, or freeze for up to 2 months.

Chicken Pumpkin Cups

Makes 6 regular or 12 small treats

These easy little treats work in either a regular 6-cup muffin tin or a 12-cup mini muffin tin. This recipe is perfect when you have one leftover chicken breast. You can use either cooked fresh pumpkin or plain canned pumpkin for this recipe, but don't use pumpkin pie filling—your dog doesn't need sugar.

1 cup milk

2 eggs

2 tablespoons molasses

¼ teaspoon ground cinnamon

¼ teaspoon ground ginger

¼ teaspoon sea salt

¾ cup cooked fresh or canned pumpkin

1 cooked chicken breast, about 8 ounces

1. Preheat the oven to 325 degrees. Spray a regular or mini muffin tin with cooking spray.

2. Heat the milk on the stove or microwave until it is steaming but not boiling. Remove from the heat.

3. In a large bowl, beat the eggs lightly. Add the molasses, cinnamon, ginger, and salt. Beat thoroughly to combine. Stir in the pumpkin, followed by the warm milk.

4. Carefully spoon the pumpkin mixture into the prepared baking cups. Cut the chicken breast into 6 or 12 pieces, depending on the size of the muffin tin you are using. Put a piece of chicken in the middle of each cup, so the pumpkin custard covers it.

5. Bake the custards about 30 minutes for regular muffin tins, about 20 minutes for mini muffin tins—or until the custard looks set and doesn't jiggle when gently shaken. Remove the custards from the oven and cool completely on a wire rack. Remove carefully with a small spatula and serve at room temperature, or refrigerate, covered, and serve within 2 days. Freeze leftovers in an airtight container for up to 2 months.

Cheese Yips

Makes 12 regular or 24 small treats

These cheesy wafers contain just one ingredient. (Yes, cheese, of course!) I first learned how to do this when researching for a book I coauthored on Mediterranean cuisine (for people, not dogs), and I couldn't believe how the cheese behaved when I cooked it like this. Try it—these make delicious treats for dogs or people.

These taste best if you use a fresh wedge of Parmesan and grate it yourself. They also bake best on a nonstick bakery mat, such as a Silpat sheet (a lot of companies make something similar), or on parchment paper, but you can also use a nonstick baking sheet.

1 cup grated Parmesan cheese
Peanut butter or meat paste, for filling (optional)

1. Preheat the oven to 375 degrees. Cover 2 baking sheets with nonstick bakery mats or parchment paper, or use baking sheets coated with a nonstick finish.

2. Pile the cheese in 12 two-inch or 24 one-inch circles, leaving about 3 inches between each circle. Bake just until the very edges of the cheese start to turn golden, about 5 minutes. Watch them carefully so they don't burn.

3. Remove the pan from the oven and set the baking sheet on a rack to cool. After about 2 minutes, carefully remove the yips from the baking sheet or mat with a sharp spatula or knife. Transfer to paper towels to drain off some of the grease. You can leave them flat, or roll them into a tube or cone shape while they are still warm and, after they cool, fill them with peanut butter or meat paste. Store in an airtight container in the refrigerator for up to 2 days, or freeze for up to 2 months.

Turkey Jerky

Makes about 16 large or 32 small treats

These meaty treats make dogs very happy. Similar to jerky, they dry out in the oven on low heat for several hours. However, because you start with cooked rather than raw turkey, you don't have to worry about bacterial contamination. This recipe also works well with chicken.

1 piece (about 8 ounces) cooked turkey breast

1. Preheat the oven to 175 degrees. Spray a baking sheet with nonstick cooking spray.

2. Slice the turkey breast with the grain into very thin strips (maximum ¼-inch thick). Put the strips on the baking sheet so they lie flat and don't touch one another.

3. Bake for 4 hours, or until the turkey looks dry and chewy. Remove it from the oven and cool to room temperature before serving. Store in the refrigerator for up to 3 days, or in the freezer up to 3 months.

Tofu Cubes

Makes 128 treats

This treat is super easy to make, and if you consider the cost of one pound of extra-firm tofu, it's a very cost-effective, high-protein, grain-free, meat-free treat. The draining and baking both take a long time, but it's time you can spend doing other things, so it doesn't feel time-consuming. You want to press and then bake as much moisture as possible out of these treats to make them chewier and more interesting to eat. And though 128 treats sounds like a lot, these cubes freeze well, so you can just make a batch, freeze it, and thaw enough for a few days at a time when you need them.

Dogs don't demand high flavor, so you don't need to marinate the tofu as long as you would if these treats were for you (although personally, I think these are yummy and I eat them just the way they are). You can be creative in how you season them—just remember to keep all the ingredients dog friendly (for a list of foods to avoid, see page 15).

1 pound extra-firm tofu

For the marinade (optional):
¼ cup low-sodium soy sauce or tamari
¼ cup apple juice
1 tablespoon grated fresh ginger, or 1 teaspoon ground
¼ teaspoon garlic powder

1. Press the block of tofu between layers of paper towels to get out as much moisture as you can. Cut the block into about 128 cubes (more or less, depending on how big you want the treats to be). Put a clean, smooth dish towel, cloth napkin, or several layers of paper towels on a baking sheet. Spread out the tofu cubes in a single layer. Top with another towel, napkin, or more paper towels. Put a cutting board or other flat surface over the cubes and put a heavy weight like a cast-iron pan on top of the board to help remove more moisture from the cubes. Let them press for 30 minutes to 1 hour.

2. Meanwhile, in a large shallow bowl or pan with sides, combine the soy sauce, apple juice, ginger, and garlic powder. When they've finished pressing, put the cubes in the marinade and toss to lightly coat. Put the marinating tofu in the refrigerator, covered, for at least 15 minutes to as long as overnight.

3. When the tofu is marinated, preheat the oven to 300 degrees. Spray a baking sheet with cooking spray.

4. Place the tofu cubes on the prepared baking sheet in a single layer so none of them are touching one another. Bake for 30 minutes, turn the cubes over, and bake for an additional 30 minutes, or until the cubes look dry, golden-brown, and a little bit puffed up.

5. Cool the cubes completely before serving. Store the treats in the freezer in an airtight container. Shake the container every 30 minutes as they begin to freeze to keep the cubes from sticking together, or freeze them in a single layer on the baking sheet before transferring them to the container.

Liver Snaps

Makes about 24 treats

Dogs love liver, and poultry liver is a great treat because it is so nutrient-dense. It's a food dogs would choose to eat in the wild, all on their own. In this recipe, the liver is cooked first, then dried like jerky.

2 fresh chicken livers (about 3 ounces)
1 tablespoon anise or fennel seeds
1-inch piece fresh ginger, peeled and sliced
4 cups low-sodium chicken broth or water

1. Put the chicken livers in a soup pot or large saucepan. Sprinkle with the anise or fennel seeds and ginger slices, then add the broth or water. Bring to a boil and boil for 15 minutes, or until the liver is cooked through (it will turn grayish-brown).

2. Preheat the oven to 200 degrees. Spray a baking sheet with cooking spray.

3. Drain the livers, discarding the broth and spices. Slice each liver into 12 slices (more or less). Arrange the liver slices on the prepared baking sheet so they don't touch one another. Bake for 3 hours, or until the liver slices are dry and crisp. Store in an airtight container in the refrigerator for up to 2 days, or in the freezer up to 2 months.

CHAPTER ELEVEN

What's for Dessert?

~

Dogs don't need dessert.
In fact, they probably don't even want dessert. They would rather
finish off your cheeseburger. But the treats in this chapter
aren't desserts in the way we think of them. They don't contain any white sugar,
white flour, or high fructose corn syrup, but they are a little bit sweet,
because many dogs do enjoy a sweet taste. The only sweeteners
in these recipes are honey, molasses, or fresh fruit—and only a little,
because that's all dogs should have.

The main reason for having a dessert chapter, quite frankly,
is for you. I know I like to make dessert, and I'm guessing
you do, too. So live it up and make these pretty confections for
your hungry pup. You can feel good feeding him these treats,
rather than those sugar- and preservative-laden treats
from the grocery store.

Double Carob Chip Cookies

Makes 12 regular or 24 small cookies

Dogs can't eat chocolate, but they *can* eat carob, which is similar in taste and texture. You can buy carob powder and carob chips in your local health food store and in the health food aisle of your grocery store. These carob-y cookies aren't very sweet, but they are very delicious.

½ cup unsalted butter, softened, or non-hydrogenated margarine
(like Earth Balance)

¼ cup honey

1 cup whole-wheat pastry flour

½ cup carob powder

½ teaspoon baking soda

¾ cup carob chips

1. Preheat the oven to 350 degrees. Spray a baking sheet with cooking spray.

2. In a large bowl, use an electric mixer or a wooden spoon to beat the butter or margarine and honey together until well combined.

3. In a separate bowl, stir together the flour, carob powder, and baking soda. Add the flour mixture to the butter mixture, beating until the ingredients are completely incorporated. Stir in the carob chips.

4. Roll pieces of the dough into 12 one-inch or 24 half-inch balls (depending on your size preference) and arrange them about 1 inch apart on the prepared baking sheet. Bake for 12 minutes, or about 8 minutes for the smaller size—or until the cookies just start to turn golden.

5. Remove the cookies from the oven and cool on a wire rack for 15 minutes or until completely cooled. Store the cookies in an airtight container in the refrigerator for up to 4 days, or in the freezer for up to 4 months.

———

Crunchy Apple Crisp

Makes 16 regular or 32 small treats

This fruity treat bakes up just like the apple crisps you probably know and love, except this one is sugar-free. Just cut it into squares and serve.

½ cup unsalted butter
3 cooking apples (like Granny Smith), peeled, cored, and thinly sliced
Juice from 1 lemon (about 2 tablespoons)

1 cup nonfat plain yogurt
1 cup rolled oats
½ cup cornmeal
½ cup ground flaxseeds
¼ cup ground almonds
1 tablespoon anise seeds, crushed or ground
½ teaspoon ground cinnamon
½ teaspoon dried ginger

1. Preheat the oven to 375 degrees. Rub 1 tablespoon of the butter on the inside of an 8-inch square baking pan.

2. Toss the apples with the lemon juice, then arrange the slices in the bottom of the prepared pan. Spread with the yogurt.

3. In a large bowl or in a food processor, combine the oats, cornmeal, flaxseeds, almonds, anise seeds, cinnamon, and ginger. Cut in the remaining 7 tablespoons of butter with a pastry cutter, or pulse until the mixture resembles coarse crumbs. Sprinkle the mixture evenly over the yogurt.

4. Bake for 45 minutes, or until the apples are soft and the crust turns golden brown. Cool completely and slice into squares. Store in an airtight container in the refrigerator for up to 2 days, or in the freezer for up to 2 months.

Ricotta Cupcakes

Makes 12 regular or 24 mini cupcakes

These whole-grain cupcakes have a cheesy surprise in the center.

1 cup unsweetened applesauce

½ cup olive oil

½ cup honey

1 egg

½ cup ground flaxseeds

1 teaspoon baking soda

1½ cups whole-wheat pastry flour

¾ cup part-skim ricotta cheese

1. Preheat the oven to 375 degrees. Spray a muffin tin with cooking spray, or line with paper liners.

2. In a large bowl, combine the applesauce, olive oil, honey, egg, flaxseeds, and baking soda. Mix well. Stir in the flour and mix until completely combined.

3. Fill each muffin cup a little less than half full. Put 1 tablespoon (for standard cups) or half a tablespoon (for mini cups) of ricotta cheese in the middle of each cupcake. Top with remaining batter.

4. Bake for 20 minutes, or about 10 minutes for mini muffins—or until the cupcakes turn golden brown. Cool on a wire rack for 15 minutes before serving. Store in an airtight container in the refrigerator for up to 2 days, or in the freezer for up to 2 months.

Beef Brûlée

Makes I regular or 2 small treats

If you want to get technical about it, this isn't really brûlée because it doesn't have a burnt sugar topping, it's not nearly as rich (which wouldn't be healthy for your pup), and it's a lot easier to make! I'm taking liberties with the term, but I don't think your dog will mind. Nevertheless, this is a rich treat, so save it for special occasions. If you have a large dog, make the larger size. If you have one or two small dogs, the small size is just right.

To serve these, just give your dog the ramekin and let him eat out of it like he would any other bowl. You don't mind, do you? If you do, consider buying a few ramekins just for your dog. Mark them with a permanent marker if you want to keep them separate. You could write your dog's name on his own personal ramekin, or you could draw a little paw-print on it. Personally, I just put them in the dishwasher. I'm confident that they come out perfectly clean.

¼ cup heavy cream

1 whole egg

½ cup minced cooked beef

1. Preheat the oven to 300 degrees.

2. In a large bowl, combine the cream and egg. Beat lightly.

3. Stir in the beef.

4. Pour the mixture into 1 regular or 2 small ramekins or custard dishes. Put the ramekin in a baking pan with high sides and carefully pour hot water into the pan so it's level with the custard in the ramekins, being careful not to get any water into the custard.

5. Bake for 45 minutes, or about 30 minutes for the smaller size, or until the custard is set in the middle. Carefully remove the brûlée from the water and cool completely on a wire rack. Serve, or cover and refrigerate for up to 2 days. (This dish does not freeze well.)

Chicken Pudding Cups

Makes 1 regular or 2 small treats

This recipe is more like an old-fashioned Yorkshire pudding than the kind of pudding Americans are used to eating. But, like the Beef Brûlée recipe (page 116), it bakes in individual ramekins or custard cups.

1 egg
½ cup milk
¼ cup whole-wheat pastry flour
½ cup minced cooked chicken

1. Preheat the oven to 450 degrees.

2. In a bowl, beat the egg lightly. Stir in the milk. Add the flour and mix until well combined. Stir in the chicken.

3. Pour the batter into 1 regular or 2 small ramekins or custard dishes. Transfer the ramekins to a large pan with sides, put the pan into the oven, and then carefully pour hot water into the pan so it's just level with the custard in the ramekins. Be careful not to get any water into the custard.

4. Bake for 10 minutes, then lower the oven temperature to 350 degrees. Bake for an additional 15 minutes for regular-size ramekins or 10 minutes for small ramekins—or until the puddings puff up and turn brown.

5. Remove the puddings from the oven and cool completely on a wire rack. Serve, or cover and refrigerate for up to 2 days. (Does not freeze well.)

Pooch Petit Fours

Makes 20 large or 40 small treats

Petit fours—little tea cakes made to be eaten in one or two bites—make excellent dog treats, as long as they aren't made with a lot of white flour and sugar. These aren't. This recipe uses the same base as the Ricotta Cupcakes (page 115), but these treats are "frosted" with a cream cheese/butter glaze.

1 cup unsweetened applesauce
½ cup olive oil
½ cup honey
1 egg
½ cup ground flaxseeds
1 teaspoon baking soda
1½ cups whole-wheat pastry flour
4 ounces cream cheese, softened
2 tablespoons butter, softened
2 tablespoons canola oil
2 tablespoons molasses

1. Preheat the oven to 350 degrees. Spray a 13 x 9–inch baking pan with cooking spray.

2. In a large bowl, combine the applesauce, olive oil, honey, egg, flaxseeds, and baking soda. Mix well. Stir in the flour and mix until completely combined.

3. Pour the batter into the baking pan. Bake for 30 minutes, or until the cake turns golden brown and a toothpick inserted in the center comes out clean. Cool completely on a wire rack, then cut into 20 to 40 squares, depending on your size preference. Put the squares on a baking rack with wax paper underneath to catch the icing.

4. In a medium-sized bowl, combine the cream cheese, butter, canola oil, molasses, and ¼ cup water. Beat until smooth. The icing should be thick, but you should be able to pour it. If it is too thick, add a little more water, 1 teaspoon at a time.

5. Dip each cake square into the icing and set it back on the rack to dry (this can get messy). Drizzle any remaining icing evenly over the squares. Let the icing set, then refrigerate in an airtight container for up to 2 days, or freeze for up to 2 months.

Honey Hush Puppies

Makes 12 regular or 24 small treats

Traditional hush puppies are deep-fried in fat, but nobody needs that. This baked version is different in other ways, too—it's sweetened with honey, making it a treat dogs will love to have for dessert. For a non-dessert variation, omit the honey and add a half cup of minced cooked fish instead.

1 cup cornmeal

½ cup whole-wheat pastry flour

¼ cup ground flaxseeds or ground almonds

2 teaspoons baking powder

½ teaspoon baking soda

½ teaspoon sea salt

½ teaspoon anise or fennel seeds

½ teaspoon ground ginger

½ teaspoon garlic powder

½ cup honey

3 egg whites

1. Preheat the oven to 400 degrees. Spray 2 baking sheets with cooking spray.

2. In a large bowl, combine the cornmeal, flour, flaxseeds or almonds, baking powder, baking soda, salt, anise or fennel seeds, ginger, and garlic powder.

3. In a separate bowl, beat the honey and the egg whites together until the egg whites just start to thicken. Add the honey mixture to the cornmeal mixture and mix thoroughly.

4. Using your hands, form the dough into 12 to 24 balls, depending on your size preference. Put the balls on the prepared baking sheet, spaced about 2 inches apart.

5. Bake the hush puppies for 15 minutes, or about 8 minutes for the small size—or until they turn golden brown. Remove the pan from the oven and allow the hush puppies to cool for at least 20 minutes before serving. Store in an airtight container in the refrigerator for up to 3 days, or in the freezer for up to 3 months.

Fido's Favorite Frozen Yogurt

Makes 24 frozen treats

Some dogs go crazy for frozen treats, and a handful of companies have started marketing frozen treats of all types for dogs. Freeze these treats in an ice cube tray, then pop them out when you're ready to serve them. Toss one in your dog's bowl and see what happens. Not all dogs like frozen treats, but the ones that do will lick and lick and lick, happy and content until the frozen treat is gone.

¾ cup nonfat plain yogurt
½ cup low-sodium chicken, turkey, or beef broth
½ cup fresh or frozen blueberries

Combine the yogurt, broth, and blueberries in a blender, and blend until smooth. Freeze in ice cube trays until hard. Serve. Store (obviously!) in the freezer.

{CHAPTER TWELVE}

Happy Holidays for Hounds, and Other Canine Celebrations

~

*Dogs love routine, and the holidays can get stressful
for them—especially if you travel a lot, or if you have visitors coming
in and out of the house, or if you get all stressed out. Pets mirror
our own emotions, so do your pet a favor:
Take a deep breath, chill out, and go bake something.
I know it always relaxes me.*

*Remember, too, that a lot of the holiday goodies
people eat are not safe or good for pets. Instead, bake these just-for-pet holiday
treats, and your dog can celebrate the season right along with you.*

Spring Chicken Cakes

Makes 20 regular or 40 small treats

When the weather finally starts to warm up in the spring, the crocuses push up through the snow, and the first buds appear on the ends of tree branches, it's time to make this cake.

1 cup rolled oats
½ cup canola oil
1 cup minced cooked chicken
½ cup minced baby greens (like collards, chard, or kale)
½ cup fresh or frozen baby peas
1 cup whole-wheat pastry flour
½ cup unsweetened flaked or grated coconut
1 teaspoon baking soda
½ teaspoon sea salt
3 eggs

1. Preheat the oven to 350 degrees. Spray a 13 x 9–inch baking pan with cooking spray.
2. Boil 1½ cups of water in a saucepan or teapot. When the water boils, add it to the oats and let it sit for 10 minutes, then stir in the canola oil, chicken, greens, and peas.

3. In a separate bowl, stir together the flour, coconut, baking soda, and salt, until well combined.

4. Using an electric mixer or beating vigorously by hand, add the flour mixture and the eggs to the oats in the following order: a third of the flour mixture, 1 egg, half the remaining flour mixture, the second egg, the remaining flour mixture, and the remaining egg. Beat until well combined.

5. Pour the batter into the prepared baking pan. Bake for 30 minutes, or until the cake turns golden brown and a toothpick inserted into the center comes out clean. Remove the cake from the oven and cool completely on a wire rack.

6. Cut the cake into squares and serve. Store leftovers in an airtight container in the refrigerator for up to 2 days, or in the freezer for up to 2 months.

Bow-Wow Birthday Cake

Makes 12 regular or 24 small treats

It's your dog's birthday? What better way to celebrate is there than with a very special peanut butter–banana cake oh-so-subtly scented with chicken and livers, baked just for your favorite birthday dog?

1½ cups whole-wheat pastry flour

1 teaspoon baking soda

⅓ cup natural peanut butter

1 (4-ounce) jar strained chicken baby food

2 tablespoons peanut oil

1 cup peeled, mashed, very ripe bananas (about 2 large or 3 medium bananas)

2 eggs

2 chicken livers, boiled until cooked through

4 ounces cream cheese, softened

¼ cup nonfat plain yogurt, plus more as needed

Freshly cut carrot sticks (as garnish, to replace candles)

1. Preheat the oven to 350 degrees. Spray an 8-inch round cake pan with cooking spray.

2. In a large bowl, mix together the flour and baking soda. Stir in the peanut butter, baby food, peanut oil, bananas, and eggs. Mix until thoroughly combined.

3. Pour the batter into the cake pan and bake for 30 minutes, or until the cake turns golden brown and a toothpick inserted into the center comes out clean. Remove the cake from the oven and cool on a wire rack for about 15 minutes. Carefully turn the cake out of the pan and cool completely. Invert the cake onto a serving plate.

4. Puree the chicken livers in a blender or food processor, or mince them with a sharp knife. In a medium-sized bowl, combine the livers, cream cheese, and yogurt. Mix thoroughly, or beat with an electric mixer until completely combined. If the mixture is too thick to spread easily, mix in more yogurt.

5. Frost the cake with the cream cheese–liver mixture. Insert carrot sticks into the cake as you would candles. Serve with revelry! Store leftovers in an airtight container in the refrigerator for up to 2 days, or in the freezer for up to 2 months.

Red, White, and Blue Bones

Makes about 30 cookies

These patriotic dog biscuits make the perfect Independence Day snack. Plus, since midsummer is flea season, these biscuits contain yeast, which some people believe repels fleas. Some also say that garlic repels fleas, but since fresh garlic could be toxic to your dog, use only a small amount of garlic powder instead.

1 cup whole-wheat pastry flour

¼ cup ground flaxseeds

¼ cup brewer's or nutritional yeast

½ teaspoon sea salt

2 tablespoons olive oil

1 teaspoon garlic powder

⅔ cup low-sodium chicken broth

¼ cup fresh or frozen thawed, blueberries, well mashed with a fork

¼ cup fresh or frozen (thawed) strawberries, well mashed with a fork

¼ cup nonfat plain yogurt

1 teaspoon cornstarch

1. Preheat the oven to 400 degrees. Cover 2 baking sheets with nonstick bakery mats or parchment paper, or use baking sheets coated with a nonstick finish.

2. In a large bowl, combine the flour, flaxseeds, yeast, and salt.

3. In a separate bowl, whisk together the olive oil, garlic powder, and broth. Add the oil mixture to the flour mixture slowly, mixing with a fork as you pour. Once the oil mixture has been incorporated, divide the dough into three equal parts.

4. Knead one section of dough a few times and set it aside. Add the blueberries to another section of dough, kneading them into the dough with your hands. If the dough is too sticky, add a little bit more flour until it feels just dry enough to roll out without sticking. Set the blueberry dough aside. Add the strawberries to the final section of dough in the same manner as the blueberries.

5. On a well-floured surface, roll out the blue dough to a ¼-inch thickness and cut into bone-shaped cookies with a cookie cutter or freehand, with a sharp knife. Carefully transfer the cutouts onto the cookie sheet. Repeat with the strawberry dough, then again with the plain dough. Brush the yogurt onto the plain dough biscuits, and dust them lightly with cornstarch.

6. Bake the cookies 15 minutes, then turn off the heat and leave the cookies in the oven for 1 hour (with the oven door closed).

7. Remove the cookies from the oven and serve. Store leftovers in an air-tight container in the refrigerator for up to 4 days, or in the freezer for up to 4 months.

―――――――

Boo-tiful Halloween Bread

Makes 1 regular or 2 mini loaves

This Halloween-y treat might also trick any humans who try it. It's pumpkin bread—but it also contains ground turkey!

1 cup whole-wheat pastry flour

½ cup ground flaxseeds

1 teaspoon baking soda

1 cup cooked fresh or canned (unsweetened) pumpkin puree

½ cup olive oil

2 eggs, lightly beaten

¼ cup low-sodium chicken broth

½ teaspoon cinnamon

1 cup cooked ground turkey, finely broken up

½ cup carob chips

1. Preheat the oven to 350 degrees. Spray a loaf pan with cooking spray.

2. In a large bowl, mix the flour, flaxseeds, and baking soda together until thoroughly combined. In a separate bowl, mix the pumpkin, olive oil, eggs, chicken broth, and cinnamon until thoroughly combined. Add the pumpkin mixture to the flour mixture, and stir until just combined. Don't overmix—the batter will be lumpy.

3. Fold in the ground turkey and carob chips. Pour the batter into the prepared loaf pan. Bake for 1 hour, or until the bread looks nicely browned and a toothpick inserted into the middle comes out clean.

4. Remove the bread from the oven and cool completely on a wire rack. Cut the bread into slices or cubes for treats. Store leftovers in an airtight container in the refrigerator for up to 2 days, or in the freezer up to 2 months.

Thanksgiving Dinner Pie

Makes 12 regular or 24 small treats

Sick of those Thanksgiving leftovers? Cook them up in a pie and let your dog help share the burden. If your bread stuffing is full of onions, use a frozen whole-wheat piecrust for a single-crust pie instead of the stuffing, since onions can be toxic to dogs.

3 cups leftover bread stuffing (see note above)

2 cups cooked turkey, coarsely chopped

1 cup cooked mixed vegetables (green beans, peas, corn, sweet potatoes, or whatever you have left over from Thanksgiving)

½ cup low-sodium turkey gravy (without onions)

2 cups mashed potatoes

1 teaspoon paprika

1. Preheat the oven to 350 degrees. Spray a 9-inch pie plate with cooking spray.
2. Press the bread stuffing into the pie plate to form a crust. Top with the turkey. Mash the cooked vegetables with a fork and sprinkle them over the turkey, then pour the gravy over the vegetables. Frost the pie with the mashed potatoes, and sprinkle the top with paprika.

3. Bake for 45 minutes, or until heated through. Cool on a wire rack for 20 minutes, then cut into individual treat-sized servings. Cover leftovers and store in the refrigerator for up to 2 days, or in the freezer for up to 2 months.

Pumpkin Puffs

Makes 12 regular or 24 small popovers

 (broth)

These fresh-from-the-oven, pumpkin-infused popovers are a great treat on a crisp fall morning. Be sure to use whole-wheat pastry flour, not regular whole-wheat flour.

¼ cup cooked fresh or canned (unsweetened) pumpkin puree

3 whole eggs

3 egg whites

2 cups low-sodium chicken or beef broth

2 tablespoons canola oil

2 cups whole-wheat pastry flour

½ teaspoon salt

¼ teaspoon ground ginger

1. Preheat the oven to 400 degrees. Put muffin tins with space for making either 12 regular or 24 mini muffins on a baking sheet in the oven as it preheats.

2. In a large bowl, combine the pumpkin, eggs, egg whites, broth, and canola oil. Whip the mixture briefly with a wire whisk until the color lightens slightly.

3. In a separate bowl, combine the flour, salt, and ginger. Add the pumpkin mixture to the flour mixture and whisk the whole thing together until all the ingredients are thoroughly incorporated.

4. Remove the muffin tins from the oven and spray the cups with cooking spray. Quickly fill the cups with the batter and return them to the oven.

5. Bake the popovers for 25 minutes, or 15 minutes for the mini size—or until they puff up and turn golden brown. Take the puffs out of the oven and pierce each one with a sharp knife to release the steam. Return the popovers to the oven and bake for 5 more minutes.

6. Remove the tins from the oven and cool on wire racks for at least 15 minutes before serving. Store in an airtight container in the refrigerator for up to 2 days, or in the freezer for up to 2 months.

Turkey Tail Turnovers

Makes 18 regular or 36 small turnovers

This recipe uses Puppy Pastry Dough to make fan-shaped turnovers that look like turkey tails. This is another good way to use up leftover turkey after a big Thanksgiving feast.

1 cup chopped cooked turkey
¼ cup cooked or canned creamed corn
¼ cup nonfat plain yogurt
¼ teaspoon sea salt
¼ teaspoon garlic powder
1 batch Puppy Pastry Dough (page 80)

1. Preheat the oven to 350 degrees. Spray 2 baking sheets with cooking spray.

2. In a medium-sized bowl, combine the turkey, creamed corn, yogurt, salt, and garlic powder.

3. Divide the pastry dough in half. On a well-floured surface, roll out half the dough to a ¼-inch thickness. Carefully cut it into 9 large or 18 small circles (depending on the size of the treats you prefer to make). For larger treats, put about 2 tablespoons of the turkey mixture onto each piece of dough; for smaller treats, about 1 tablespoon. Using a brush or your fingers, moisten the edges of each turnover, then carefully fold the

dough over the filling. Press the edges with your fingers to seal, then use a sharp knife to cut the edges of the turnovers into a scalloped shape, or press with the tines of a fork. Repeat with the other half of the dough.

4. Using a spatula, carefully transfer the turnovers to the prepared baking sheets. Bake for 20 minutes, or about 10 minutes for the small size—or until golden brown. Allow the turnovers to cool on a rack for at least 30 minutes before serving—that filling inside can be hot, and you don't want anybody to burn a tongue! When the turnovers have cooled completely, store them in an airtight container in the refrigerator for up to 2 days, or freeze them for up to 2 months.

———————

Mutt Macaroons

Makes 12 regular or 24 small cookies

This is a great way to finish off a carton of egg whites, especially since meringue whips up better if the egg whites are a few days old. Don't expect these to be like candy-sweet divinity though; this "candy" doesn't contain any sugar.

3 egg whites, at room temperature

½ teaspoon cream of tartar

¼ cup finely ground almonds

¼ cup flaked or finely shredded unsweetened coconut

1. Preheat the oven to 350 degrees. Cover 2 baking sheets with nonstick bakery mats or parchment paper, or use baking sheets coated with a nonstick finish.

2. Using an electric mixer with a wire whisk (or do it manually if you have a lot of endurance and arm strength), beat the egg whites and cream of tartar until they form stiff peaks. Gently fold in the almonds and coconut with a rubber spatula.

3. Drop the meringue mixture onto the cookie sheets by tablespoons or teaspoons, depending on how large you want the treats to be. Bake for 20 minutes, or about 12 minutes for the small size—or until the meringues turn golden brown. Be careful not to burn them.

4. Remove the pans from the oven and let the macaroons cool completely before removing from the pan with a metal spatula. Store leftovers in an airtight container in the refrigerator for up to 2 days, or in the freezer up to 2 months.

Christmas Mincemeat Muffins

Makes 12 regular or 24 mini muffins

These moist, rich muffins make a delicious Christmas treat, especially because *you* make the mincemeat so you know it's safe. Don't give regular mincemeat to dogs because it contains alcohol and raisins, both of which can be toxic to dogs. This version uses cranberries and leftover sweet potatoes, and makes enough so that you'll have some for your dog and some to give away as holiday gifts to all your dog friends.

1 organic lemon
1 cup fresh or frozen finely chopped cranberries
2 apples, peeled, cored, and finely chopped
1 cup minced cooked beef
½ cup mashed sweet potatoes
½ cup molasses
1 cup whole-wheat pastry flour
½ teaspoon baking soda
½ teaspoon cinnamon

1. Preheat the oven to 350 degrees. Spray regular or mini muffin tins with cooking spray, or line with paper liners.

2. Grate the peel from the lemon into a small bowl, then squeeze all of its juice into the bowl.

3. In a large bowl, combine the cranberries, apples, beef, sweet potatoes, molasses, and the lemon peel and juice.

4. In a separate bowl, combine the flour, baking soda, and cinnamon. Add the dry mixture to the fruit-and-meat mixture and mix thoroughly.

5. Spoon the batter into the muffin cups and bake for 30 minutes, or about 15 minutes for mini muffins—or until the tops turn golden brown. Let cool for 15 minutes, then remove the muffins from the tins. Store in an airtight container in the refrigerator for up to 2 days, or freeze for up to 2 months.

Metric Conversion Charts

The recipes in this book use the standard United States method for measuring liquid and dry or solid ingredients (teaspoons, tablespoons, and cups). The information on this chart is provided to help cooks outside the U.S. successfully use these recipes. All equivalents are approximate.

Metric Equivalents for Different Types of Ingredients

A standard cup measure of a dry or solid ingredient will vary in weight depending on the type of ingredient. A standard cup of liquid is the same volume for any type of liquid. Use the following chart when converting standard cup measures to grams (weight) or milliliters (volume).

Standard Cup	Fine Powder (e.g., flour)	Grain (e.g., rice)	Granular (e.g., sugar)	Liquid Solids (e.g., butter)	Liquid (e.g., milk)
1	140 g	150 g	190 g	200 g	240 ml
¾	105 g	113 g	143 g	150 g	180 ml
⅔	93 g	100 g	125 g	133 g	160 ml
½	70 g	75 g	95 g	100 g	120 ml
⅓	47 g	50 g	63 g	67 g	80 ml
¼	35 g	38 g	48 g	50 g	60 ml
⅛	18 g	19 g	24 g	25 g	30 ml

Useful Equivalents for Liquid Ingredients by Volume

¼ tsp =				1 ml
½ tsp =				2 ml
1 tsp =				5 ml
3 tsp =	1 tblsp =		½ fl oz =	15 ml
	2 tblsp =	⅛ cup =	1 fl oz =	30 ml
	4 tblsp =	¼ cup =	2 fl oz =	60 ml
	5⅓ tblsp =	⅓ cup =	3 fl oz =	80 ml

8 tblsp =	½ cup =		4 fl oz =	120 ml
10⅔ tblsp =	⅔ cup =		5 fl oz =	160 ml
12 tblsp =	¾ cup =		6 fl oz =	180 ml
16 tblsp =	1 cup =		8 fl oz =	240 ml
	1 pt =	2 cups =	16 fl oz =	480 ml
	1 qt =	4 cups =	32 fl oz =	960 ml
			33 fl oz =	1000 ml = 1 l

Useful Equivalents for Dry Ingredients by Weight

(To convert ounces to grams, multiply the number
of ounces by 30.)

1 oz =	¹⁄₁₆ lb =	30 g		12 oz =	¾ lb =	360 g
4 oz =	¼ lb =	120 g		16 oz =	1 lb =	480 g
8 oz =	½ lb =	240 g				

Useful Equivalents for Cooking/Oven Temperatures

	Farenheit	Celcius	Gas Mark
Freeze Water	32° F	0° C	
Room Temperature	68° F	20° C	
Boil Water	212° F	100° C	
Bake	325° F	160° C	3
	350° F	180° C	4
	375° F	190° C	5
	400° F	200° C	6
	425° F	220° C	7
	450° F	230° C	8
Broil		Grill	

Useful Equivalents for Length

(To convert inches to centimeters, multiply the number of inches by 2.5.)

1 in =			2.5 cm	
6 in =	½ ft =		15 cm	
12 in =	1 ft =		30 cm	
36 in =	3 ft =	1 yd =	90 cm	
40 in =			100 cm =	1 m

Index